THE WURMBRAND FAMILY

Imprisoned for Christ

THE VOICE OF THE MARTYRS

D1066164

Living Sacrifice Book Company
Bartlesville, OK 74005

Imprisoned for Christ

Living Sacrifice Book Company
P.O. Box 2273
Bartlesville, OK 74005-2273

ISBN 978-0-88264-017-4

Cover, page design, and production by Genesis Group

Inside illustrations: Faith Ann Rumm, Rumm Studios

Printed in the United States of America

Unless otherwise indicated, Scripture references are from the *New King James* version, © 1979, 1980, 1982 by Thomas Nelson Inc., Publishers, Nashville, Tennessee.

Scripture quotations designated NIV are from the *New International Version,* © 1973, 1978, 1984 by the International Bible Society. Published by Zondervan Bible Publishers, Grand Rapids, Michigan.

To the Rev. Michael Wurmbrand,
who has lived his life in a fishbowl among
both friends and enemies, and has done
so with dignity to the glory of God. We
are grateful for the numerous personal
interviews in which he shared his
memories with patience and enthusiasm.

This story of the Wurmbrand family is told by the family members themselves. The pictures in the text show who is telling that part of the story. You will hear from Richard Wurmbrand; his wife, Sabina; and their son, Mihai.

Pastor Richard Wurmbrand

Mrs. Sabina Wurmbrand

Mihai Wurmbrand

Some words in the text are shown in bold. More information about these words can be found in the shaded boxes within the chapter.

May you be encouraged by the story of this faithful family!

Contents

PART ONE

The Road to Prison

CHAPTER 1

A Risky Sermon

I was standing at the pulpit one Sunday when the **terrorists** appeared.

They filed silently into the back of the church and sat down. I knew by their green shirts that they were members of a terrorist group called the **Iron Guard**. No one else saw them enter.

The men, women, and children in the congregation waited eagerly for me to begin my sermon. Then I saw the guns in the strangers' hands.

I thought to myself, *If this is going to be my last sermon, it should be a good one.*

Terrorists: People who use violence or threats to try to force others to do what they want. Terrorists may want a homeland of their own, a different kind of government, or other big changes in their country or the world. Terrorism is often carried out against innocent people who are not a danger to the terrorists.

My sermon told about the hands of Jesus. I said that Jesus' hands wiped away tears and fed the hungry. His hands blessed children and healed the sick.

> **Iron Guard:** A terrorist group in Romania in the mid-1900s. The Iron Guard helped the Nazis. They opposed Jews, communists, and Protestants.

"But *you!*" I said, raising my voice. "What have *you* done with *your* hands?"

The congregation stared in amazement. Their hands held Bibles! They didn't know I was preaching to the terrorists.

"You hurt innocent people with your hands!" I thundered. "Clean your hands, you sinners!"

The Iron Guard men scowled and whispered to one another. They clutched their guns while I said a closing prayer.

The church members began to leave. Some of them glanced my way curiously. They must have been puzzled by my strange sermon. When almost everyone had left the building, I came down from the pulpit.

I quickly stepped behind a curtain, slipped through a secret door, and locked it tight.

Footsteps pounded behind me. I heard men shouting, "Where's Wurmbrand? Get him!"

Racing through hidden hallways, I found my way to a side street and escaped.

In my country of **Romania**, Christians had many enemies in those days. The Iron Guard kept trying to scare us, just as they had in church that day. The police arrested many Christians. Both the police and the Iron Guard worked with the **Nazis** who ruled the country.

Because I was a pastor, I was arrested and questioned three times. Each arrest became a lesson that prepared me for harder times to come.

Romania

Capital: Bucharest

Location: On the Black Sea in south-eastern Europe

Recent History: During Pastor Wurmbrand's time in Romania, first the Nazis, then the communists ruled his country. Under communism, the government controlled the churches. Christians who did not agree with the government were persecuted.

In 1989, Nicolae Ceausescu, a communist leader, was forced from power. From 1989 to 1999, five new church buildings opened each week. Today about 88 percent of Romanians consider themselves to be Christians, though many do not take their faith seriously.

Nazis: Adolf Hitler was the leader of Germany during World War II. His followers, and those who carried out his ideas, were called "Nazis." Hitler and his Nazi soldiers took land from other countries. Hitler caused six million people to be killed, just because they were Jews. The Nazis didn't like Christians, either.

Hitler pressured Romania to join his side in the war in the early 1940s. The people of the United States, England, Russia, France, China, and other countries all tried to stop Hitler. With so many people helping, little by little Hitler was slowed down and finally stopped.

CHAPTER 2

Answers to Bold Prayers

Later, after the Nazis lost power, a million **Russian** soldiers marched into Romania.

The Russians brought communism with them. Then a struggle began that made the problems during Nazi times seem easy.

Under communism, belief in God is forbidden or discouraged. So the Russians meant trouble for Christians.

Russia

Russia was the common name for the Union of Soviet Socialist Republics (USSR), a large communist country also called the Soviet Union. The Russian communists who came to Romania were from the USSR.

The USSR broke up in 1991, and 15 countries were formed in the breakup. Russia is the name of one of the countries. It is the largest country in the world. Moscow is its capital.

Imprisoned for Christ

But I loved the Russians! Long before they came, I had prayed, "God, send me to Russia to work as a missionary, and I won't complain afterwards if I have to spend the rest of my life in prison."

God answered my prayer. But He didn't send me on the long journey to Russia. Instead, the Russians came to me!

Of course, it could be dangerous to talk about Jesus with the Russians. Their communist leaders did not want them to learn about God. But, to me, it was worth the risk.

■ ■ ■

I felt sorry for the Russians because they were atheists. Atheists do not think God exists. I had once been an atheist.

My father died when I was nine. By the time I was fourteen, I felt sure there was no God. I read books written by atheists. They said that religion was bad. My family was **Jewish**, but we didn't follow Jewish practices, or even think much about God.

Answers to Bold Prayers

Even though I was an atheist, I was so curious about churches! If I walked past a church, I wanted to go inside.

When I did go in, I didn't understand anything. I didn't like the sermons I heard. I thought God must be like a stern school principal who would never forgive me if I disobeyed Him. I wished there was a loving God who cared about me, and I felt unhappy that He did not exist.

One day, I went into a church and saw people kneeling and saying something.

I thought, *I will kneel near them so I can hear what they say. I will say what they say, and see if something happens.*

So I prayed as they did. But nothing happened.

This disappointed me.

By the time I became a young man, all I cared about was making money to spend on parties and fun. But my mother had a different plan. She knew a family with two houses, lots of money, and a daughter. Mother decided I should marry the daughter so we could all be rich.

A family friend dropped by one day. He brought along his niece, Sabina. I told Sabina about the rich girl and about Mother's plan.

"It sounds very nice," said Sabina politely.

Jew: "Jew" can mean either a person who follows Judaism (the Jewish religion), or someone who is a descendant of the Hebrew people of Bible times. Many people who are descendants of the Hebrews believe in God and follow Judaism. Most do not. Richard and Sabina Wurmbrand were Jewish atheists who became Jewish Christians.

"Well, I don't mind the houses and the money," I explained. "It's the girl I don't care for. But if I could have a girl like you, I wouldn't want the money," I said.

I was teasing her, but I liked her. And she liked me.

Sabina and I began spending a lot of time together. We found we were a lot alike. Both our families were Jewish but ignored Jewish teachings.

We had fun at parties and didn't think about tomorrow. We thought only of ourselves.

We decided to get married. After the wedding, the parties continued. Sometimes I wondered if we were wasting our lives.

One day, I prayed to God, even though I didn't believe in Him. I said something like this:

"God, I'm sure You don't exist. But if You do, which I don't believe, it is not my duty to believe in You. It is Your duty to show Yourself to me."

Far away, someone else prayed, too. A carpenter in a village high up in the mountains of Romania prayed:

"Dear God, I have served You on earth, and I want to have a reward on earth as well as in heaven. I would like my reward to be that I will not die before I bring a Jew to Christ, because Jesus came from the Jewish people. But I am old, poor, and sick. I cannot go around looking for a Jew. There aren't any Jews in my village. Please bring a Jew to my village, and I will do my best to bring him to Christ."

Something drew me to that village. I had no reason to go to that particular one. Romania has 12,000 villages, but I went to *that one.*

The village was small, and I soon met the carpenter. When he found out I was a Jew, his eyes lit up with excitement! He believed his prayer had been answered, and he gave me a Bible to read.

But this was no ordinary Bible! The carpenter and his wife had prayed over it together for hours. They asked God to lead Sabina and me to His Son, Jesus.

I read the Bible and wept over it. I saw that I had sinned against God. My bad life had been so different from Jesus' perfect one.

I was impure; He was righteous. I was full of hate; but He loved me. I decided to turn from my life of sin and follow Jesus. When I did, He accepted me as one of His own.

Sabina was horrified when I told her I had become a Christian. "I'm still young!" she sobbed. "I want to go to parties and dances and movies, not sit and listen to sermons in churches!"

But as she learned more about Jesus, she, too, began to love Him. Parties became boring to her as she realized they were no match for the joys Jesus offered.

Sabina and I felt sorry that we had been atheists, and we wanted to save the Russians from the same sin. We studied the Bible together and prayed for guidance. And soon we weren't the only members of our little family working to reach the Russians.

CHAPTER 3

A Young Missionary

Before Sabina and I became Christians, we didn't want children. We were afraid a child would keep us from having fun.

Soon after we gave our lives to Jesus, we had a son. We named him Mihai.

"He's very beautiful," I said to Sabina. "But he only cries. When will he say something clever?"

I didn't have much experience with babies.

It wasn't long before Mihai learned to be clever. Some may have thought he was a bit too clever—maybe even rude.

By this time, I had become a pastor. One Sunday when Mihai was five, he played noisily through the entire church service. By the time we got home, I had decided to punish him.

"Do you think it is nice that the pastor's son is the one who misbehaves the most in church?" I asked.

He answered, "You think I didn't listen to the sermon. But I know every word of it."

"All right," I said. "Tell me about it."

"You preached about forgiving somebody who has sinned," he said. "And I think you ought to practice what you preach and do that right now!"

Very clever, I thought.

■ ■ ■

God and His promises were real to Mihai. Once he became dangerously ill. He needed an emergency operation. The night before the operation, we called Christian friends to gather around his bed and pray.

I sat beside my son and felt his head. It burned with fever.

"Tomorrow you are going to have an operation," I said. "It will be dangerous. It's possible that you might not live through it."

"Then I'll go to heaven!" Mihai replied happily. "Angels must have fine toys. An angel might even teach me to play the harp!"

"Well, it's not that simple," I said. "You are a sinner."

"Yes, I understand," he said. "But Jesus' blood cleanses my sins. I'm not worried—I'll be in heaven."

"That's wonderful, Mihai," I said. "Now these friends have come to pray for you. The Bible says that when someone is sick, the elders of the church should pray over him. Then he will recover. Do you believe that?"

A Young Missionary

"I believe everything the Bible says," he answered.

Our friends prayed, one after another. Then Mihai prayed:

"Thank you, God, that You are making me healthy now, and that I will soon be able to go with my father to the store to buy a new toy."

My hand rested on his chest. As he prayed, I felt his body grow cooler.

When he finished his prayer, I said to Sabina, "Take his temperature. God's miracles are measured with a ther-mometer."

Mihai's temperature had dropped. He didn't need an operation the next day.

Instead, he played outside in the yard. Several days later, we went to the toy store.

■ ■ ■

By the time he turned six, Mihai wanted to share Jesus with everyone he met.

One day in the park, Mihai noticed a man sitting on a bench reading a book.

Mihai asked, "What are you reading?"

"A **novel**," the man answered.

"You should be reading the Bible," said Mihai.

"Why?" asked the man.

Novel: A novel is a long book that tells a made-up story.

"Because it tells you how to go to heaven," Mihai explained. "See that tall man over there? He's my father. He can explain things better."

I shared the gospel with the man. He later became one of Romania's greatest Christian poets.

■ ■ ■

It was against the law to share the gospel with the Russian invaders of our country. But Mihai often had no difficulty doing what was forbidden!

Once we went on a picnic. Sabina told Mihai not to drink from a dirty stream near the picnic area. He drank anyway and had a bad sore throat for weeks.

Another time he climbed a tree that he knew he should not climb. He fell out of the tree. He was hurt badly and nearly died.

Mihai and other children often filled their pockets with small Bibles and Christian booklets. Then they played near Russian soldiers on the streets or in parks. The soldiers patted them on the head and treated them kindly.

The Russian soldiers loved children. Many of them had sons and daughters back home in Russia that they had not seen in years.

The soldiers gave Mihai and his friends candy and other treats. In return, the children gave the soldiers Bibles. It would have been dangerous for adults to give the soldiers Bibles in public. But children could get away with it. They were young missionaries to the Russians.

A Young Missionary

■ ■ ■

Still, Mihai knew what could happen to those who proclaim the name of Jesus where it is forbidden. Mihai had heard about some verses in the Book of Revelation. The verses say that those who endure struggles for their faith will one day walk with Jesus in white garments.

"Does Jesus have white robes in children's sizes?" he asked me.

I assured him that they come in all sizes. I told him the story of Tarcisius, a twelve-year-old boy who lived during the time when **Romans** persecuted early Christians:

Every day, the Christians gathered at a secret meeting place. Then they took turns going to the prison to encourage Christians who had been arrested for their faith.

One day, Tarcisius volunteered to take bread and wine to the prisoners so they could celebrate the Lord's Supper. On the way, he was stopped by some of his playmates.

Romans
Citizens of the Roman Empire. The Roman Empire was powerful from the time right before Jesus lived on earth until about 500 A.D. For two and a half centuries after Jesus' death, the Romans persecuted Christians and tried to stamp out Christianity.

"Come play with us, Tarcisius!" they called out.

"No, thank you," Tarcisius answered.

"Why not?" asked one boy as they all crowded around him. They knew Tarcisius loved to play games. But these play-mates were not Christians.

"What are you carrying?" asked another as he noticed the bundle Tarcisius held.

"I've heard he is a Christian," one boy informed the group. "Maybe he's carrying some kind of Christian secret!"

Tarcisius would not tell or show them what he carried, so they beat him up.

Surely today Tarcisius walks in white robes with Jesus.

CHAPTER 4

Russians, Watches, and Rotten Cheese

I am Mihai, the son of Pastor Wurmbrand. I'm going to tell you a little about what life was like for my family and me before Father went to prison.

Like Tarcisius, I became part of the **underground church**.

My friends and I were like sneaky little bandits. But instead of stealing from people, we gave them something.

Sometimes we went with our parents to train stations at night. The Russians had taken over all the train cars for their soldiers to ride in—even the cattle cars.

Children from different churches came along to help. As the train passed by, we threw bundles of small New Testaments into the cars through the windows.

Underground Church

Jesus said, "A servant is not greater than his master. If they persecuted Me, they will persecute you ... All these things they will do to you for My name's sake, because they do not know Him who sent Me" (John 15:20,21).

Throughout Christian history, followers of Jesus have been persecuted. Persecution can include passing laws against the spread of the gospel or giving Christians fewer rights and freedoms. Or it can be more informal, with families or communities excluding or harassing Christians.

Every day, somewhere in the world, Christians are suffering rejection, imprisonment, and even torture and death because of their faith in Christ.

In places where Christians are persecuted, many believers meet secretly in homes, woods, caves, or other hidden locations. These secret Christians are part of what is called the "underground (secret) church."

The soldiers scrambled to get the books, and we hurried away from the station before the authorities caught us.

■ ■ ■

Father and I often went to restaurants and stores to find Russians to talk to. Many were eager to learn that there was a God who loved them. Their communist leaders had not taught them this. My father could pass out about forty New Testaments in three minutes.

In one restaurant, a Russian soldier asked if he could hold me on his knee. As he picked me up, he told us about his little son at home in Russia.

Russians, Watches, and Rotten Cheese

Then the man began to cry. He hadn't been allowed to go back to Russia for years, and he missed his family. I felt sorry for him at first. But I got worried when the soldier kept hugging me harder.

What if he never lets me go? I thought. I looked at my dad, who seemed a little worried. Finally, the Russian stopped crying and put me down. Whew!

■ ■ ■

The Russians loved the watches they saw in Romania. They had never owned watches before and couldn't get enough of them.

We saw Russians with several watches on each arm. Some women soldiers hung alarm clocks around their necks.

The Russians got the watches by stealing them from Romanians. Anyone who owned a watch learned not to wear it on the street.

The soldiers stopped people and ordered, "Give me your watch!"

We had a joke we told about the watch thieves. It went like this:

A Russian soldier was walking down the street with five watches on each arm. But he didn't know what time it was because all the watches were set to different times. He passed an elderly man who was walking with a cane.

"What time is it?" the soldier asked.

Imprisoned for Christ

*The elderly man was an **astronomer**. He knew a good way to tell time on sunny days. He held his cane in such a way that it would cast a shadow. The position of the shadow told him what time it was.*

"It's 2:30," he informed the soldier.

"Give me your cane!" the soldier demanded.

> **Astronomer:** A person who is knowledgeable about the universe beyond the earth, especially heavenly bodies.

If Romanians wanted watches, they went to the Russian soldiers' barracks to buy stolen ones. Sometimes they bought back their own watches!

My father always tried to turn problems into ways to talk about Jesus with people who didn't know Him.

He went to the barracks one day, and he pretended to shop for a watch. As the soldiers crowded around him, he began to tell them Bible stories.

One of the Russians said, "You didn't come to buy watches! You came to talk to us about the Christian faith!"

Father wondered what the soldier would do next. Would he report him?

But the soldier continued, "Please sit down and talk to us. But be very careful! We know who we have to watch out for. These men around us are all good men. But when I signal you by putting my hand on your knee, you must talk only about watches. When I take my hand away, you may start preaching again."

"Thank you," Father said as he sat down with the soldiers. "Let me tell you a story from the Book of Luke. Jesus and two men were walking to a village. When they came near the village, Jesus acted as if He were going farther instead of stopping at the village with them. Why do you think He did that? Surely He wanted to go with the men."

The soldier put his hand on Father's knee. Someone he didn't trust was passing by.

"I'd rather have a watch with a brown band than a black one," said Father. "I'm willing to pay a good price."

The soldier took his hand away.

"Jesus acted as if He were going farther because He is polite," Father picked up where he left off. "He wanted to be sure the men wanted Him to stay with them. When He saw that He was welcome, He gladly entered the house with them."

"What's going on here?" asked a soldier who just joined the group. "What are you talking about?" He approached so quickly that no one had a chance to warn my father.

"Watches, of course!" answered Father. "I'm looking for a special kind that glows in the dark. Do you have one?"

"No!" growled the soldier, and he walked away.

The soldiers listening to my father smiled.

"The communists are not polite like Jesus," one whispered. "They force us to listen to them from morning to night, whether we want to or not."

Other soldiers quietly agreed. In time, some of them became followers of Jesus. With their help, Father visited the barracks many times to preach and pretend to buy watches.

■ ■ ■

My mother was a bold witness for the Lord, too. She and some of her Christian friends sang together on street corners. People gathered around them to hear the beautiful singing. Then Mother told them about Jesus. She and her friends always left the corner before the police arrived.

■ ■ ■

During these times, we were very poor. Many others in Romania were even worse off than we were. We often saw beggars begging for food.

Every morning, my parents let me crawl in bed with them. Then Father often told me stories. One day he told about a woman and a beggar:

A long time ago, a poor beggar asked a woman for food, and she gave the poor man rotten cheese.

Later, the woman went to heaven. She saw Abraham and Isaac and many others sitting at a table for a fine banquet. An angel showed her to a small table in a corner of the banquet hall.

"You may eat here," the angel said. The only food on the table was rotten cheese.

Of course, it wasn't a true story. But it stuck in my mind.

I remembered it during family devotions when we studied Luke 3:11: "He who has two tunics, let him give to him who has none; and he who has food, let him do likewise." I knew a tunic was some kind of clothing.

Father had only one suit to wear to church. The suit became old and frayed, but he still wore it.

We knew a missionary who had gone back to his home in Norway for a visit. When he returned to Romania, he brought my father some cloth for a suit!

Father was very thankful. He gave the cloth to a tailor to make a suit for him. After a while, the tailor came to our house with the new suit.

I watched as my father stood at the mirror in his new clothes, enjoying the tailor's fine work. I thought of the Bible verse about the tunics.

"Father," I said, "now you can give one of your suits to Brother Jon at the church. He doesn't have a suit. And the clothes he does have are torn and ragged."

Father stopped admiring the suit in the mirror and turned to me. "Which suit should I give him, Mihai?" he asked.

"The one you want to wear in heaven," I answered, remembering the woman who had nothing but rotten cheese to eat.

Father went to the phone and called Brother Jon. He came over and got his new suit in less than an hour.

Later, Father said it was a hard decision to give up his fine new suit. But at the time, he made it look easy to share.

I felt very proud of my father. I was sad later when he went to prison. But I never stopped being proud of him.

CHAPTER 5

The Courage to Speak

 After years of communist rule in Russia, some of the Russians acted like mindless robots.

I once asked a Russian, "Do you believe in God?"

I wouldn't have minded if he just said, "No." God gives everyone the choice whether to believe or not to believe.

But when I asked him, he looked at me blankly and said, "I don't have a military order to believe. If I am ordered to believe, I will believe."

I began to weep for him. Tears ran down my face. Here was a man whose mind had died. He had lost a great gift that God has given mankind—the gift of thinking for himself. He could not think on his own anymore.

I promised God that I would help the Russians learn to think for themselves again.

Imprisoned for Christ

■ ■ ■

The communists feared losing their power. They knew Christianity was the only thing left that had more power than they did.

When people believe in Christ, they can't be stopped from thinking for themselves. A Christian couldn't be turned into a mindless robot.

They could take away a Christian's freedom, but not his faith in God.

Communists could put a person's body in jail, but not the spirit. They could take away a Christian's freedom, but not his faith in God. The communists fought hard against the Christians because they couldn't control them.

■ ■ ■

When people joined the Communist Party, they received a Party card. Party members received special privileges.

Without a Party card, it was harder to get jobs and food. That's why millions of Romanians became communists. Christians did secret missionary work among the Romanian communists, too.

■ ■ ■

We found a new way to pass out gospel booklets to the Russian and Romanian communists. Communist officials put a seal of approval on books that pleased them. So we made booklets with pictures of Karl Marx on the cover and gave them to the officials.

Karl Marx was a dead communist hero. He believed that man has no soul. Marx said religion is "the opiate of the people." An opiate is a drug that makes people sleepy and dull.

Beside Marx's picture, we put a title: *Religion is the Opiate of the People.* The officials thought our books contained communist teachings, and they put their seal of approval on them.

Inside the booklets, after a few pages of quotes from communist heroes, we put the message of Christ. Then we went to communist meetings and offered the books for sale.

The communists saw the picture of Karl Marx and competed with each other to buy the booklets. By the time they got to page 10 and found out that the books were about God, we were far away!

■ ■ ■

We knew there was a chance we could get arrested for our tricks. Some Christians did more than take chances. They witnessed for Christ in places where they were *certain* to get arrested.

Two courageous believers once went to a government building. Many people stood outside on the steps. The crowd surrounded Gheorghiu Dej, a communist leader.

Imprisoned for Christ

The Christians pushed their way through all the people to get closer to Mr. Dej. They knew they would have only a few moments to speak with him before they were arrested.

"Christ came into the world to save you," said the first Christian to Mr. Dej.

"Turn from your sins," said the other.

"Follow Him as your Lord and Savior, and you will have eternal life," one said.

The police grabbed the Christians and dragged them away. Mr. Dej had them thrown in prison where they suffered greatly for their boldness.

Years later, Mr. Dej became very sick. He remembered what the Christians had said to him. He told God he was sorry for his sins, and he became a follower of Christ.

Not long after that he died. He went to heaven because two Christians were willing to pay the price to tell him about Jesus.

■ ■ ■

Jesus warned His followers to watch out for wolves dressed in sheep's clothing. At first the communists were kind and friendly to church leaders.

"Freedom of worship for all!" they proclaimed.

They acted like sheep. But they were really wolves.

Communist officials invited thousands of religious leaders to a meeting in the **Parliament** building. **Muslim** mullahs, Jewish rabbis, and Christian pastors and bishops crowded into the great hall. Sabina and I joined them.

Inside, red flags hung everywhere. (Red is the symbol of communism.) The top communists were seated on the stage at the front of the hall.

Behind them hung a huge picture of Joseph Stalin. The communists announced that Mr. Stalin would be the honorary president of the meeting. Bishops, rabbis, and mullahs cheered and applauded.

Sabina and I did not applaud. We knew that Stalin, a Russian communist, was the president of the World Atheist's Organization. He also persecuted Christians.

The people who applauded knew about Stalin, too. They applauded because they were scared. They were afraid of losing their jobs or going to prison.

The communist officials began their speeches.

"We want to be friends with church leaders!" said one official. "We plan to pay religious leaders and to give them raises!"

More applause.

"I am the son of a minister!" said another communist leader to the crowd. "You can count on me!"

The speeches were broadcast on the radio to the whole country. Romanians every-

Parliament: The main governing body in charge of making laws in some countries.

Muslim: A person who follows the religion of Islam. Islam was started by a man named Mohammed who was born in 570 A.D. Many of the teachings of Islam disagree with the truths in the Bible. For example, Muslims do not believe that Jesus is the Son of God, or that people are saved by grace through faith instead of by works.

where heard the pastors and other leaders cheering for communism. Some began to think that maybe communism might be a good thing for the country.

A pastor stood and walked to the microphone. "If we can count on you, then you can count on us!" he declared.

The crowd cheered. More Christians got up to speak.

"Christianity and communism have a lot in common," said one. "Both believe in ending suffering and bringing about justice. We can work together!"

"I know they are speaking out of fear," Sabina said to me. "But they could at least keep silent. They are filling the air with lies."

One leader after another rose to give their comments in support of the communists. Finally Sabina couldn't stand it anymore.

"Richard, please stand up and wash away this shame from the face of Christ," she said. "They are spitting in His face."

"If I stand up for Christ, you will lose your husband," I answered.

I knew the communists would do something terrible to me if I spoke against them.

God gave Sabina the strength to say what would give me courage.

"I don't want to have a husband who is a coward," she said.

I raised my hand to speak.

The Courage to Speak

"It is our duty to glorify God and Christ," I said when I reached the microphone. "We must first be loyal to Christ, not to earthly leaders. He is the one who died for us on the cross."

The people in the crowed seemed to wake up as from a dream. A few began to clap. Many began to cheer.

"Your right to speak is withdrawn!" shouted a communist leader.

"God gives me the right to speak," I continued. "Earthly powers come and go. Christ is eternal. Let us praise Him."

"Cut the microphone!" an official yelled.

But the crowd cheered so loudly, no one could hear him. Finally the wires to the microphone were cut and I stepped down from the stage. The shouting and clapping went on.

The meeting was over. Sabina and I made our way out of the hall through the noise and confusion. We went to the house where my mother and Mihai were listening on the radio.

"When the broadcast was cut off, I worried that I'd never see you again!" Mother said. "I thought they'd arrested both of you! What will happen now?"

"Mother," I replied, "I have a powerful Savior. He'll do what is best for me."

Later, the communists made me suffer for what I did at the meeting, but it was worth it.

Obeying the Law

The Bible tells us we should obey the authorities, "For rulers hold no terror for those who do right, but for those who do wrong" (Romans 13:3, NIV). Were the underground Christians in Romania disobeying the Bible when they found ways around the rules of the communist officials?

Peter and other apostles disobeyed the authorities who told them not to speak or teach in the name of Jesus. "We ought to obey God rather than men," said Peter and the apostles (Acts 5:29).

Moses' mother hid him from the authorities who had ordered Hebrew babies to be killed (Exodus 2).

Rahab hid the Hebrew spies against the orders of the king of Jericho (Joshua 2).

In Romans 13:5, Paul says we obey the authorities "because of conscience" (NIV). Suppose you saw a child drowning in a pond where a "No Trespassing" sign was posted. If you obeyed the sign and the child drowned, would your conscience bother you? If you saved the child, would your conscience bother you because you disobeyed the sign?

God gives each of us a conscience because, when backed up by Scripture, it helps us do His will. What is His will?

- Mark 16:15 says, "Go into all the world and preach the gospel to every creature."
- Second Peter 3:9 tells us that the Lord doesn't want anyone to perish, but all to come to repentance.
- Romans 10 asks how the lost can believe unless someone preaches to them.

The Underground Christians in Romania, and those around the world today, believe they are obeying God "rather than men."

CHAPTER 6

Staying to the End

The communists didn't try to punish me right away for speaking out. But they did send hecklers to disrupt our church meetings. Rough-looking youths pushed their way into the church hall. While I preached, they whistled, yelled, and interrupted.

I also heard rumors that the government planned to take away my license to be a pastor. Christians were not allowed to spread the gospel outside a church. But pastors could still preach inside a church if they had a license. Without a license, it would be against the law for me to preach anywhere.

■ ■ ■

The communists began arresting anyone who didn't agree with them. **Secret police** burst into homes and conducted long searches.

> **Secret Police:** A police force that usually works in secret. Governments that have secret police forces usually use them to try to control people who may not agree with the government.

"Come with us to the station to make a statement," they told people. "You don't need to bring anything. It will take only a few hours."

For many people, the "hours" turned into years.

■ ■ ■

Until this time, my life as a pastor was very satisfying. My family's needs were met. The church members loved and trusted me.

But I was not at peace. Why was my life going so well while others suffered for their faith? On many nights, Sabina and I prayed together, asking God to let us bear a cross.

■ ■ ■

One day, the police took me to their station for questioning. They didn't let me go home for three weeks.

Thousands of people were leaving Romania. They preferred living in other countries to risking arrest at home.

"It's not too late for us to leave," I told Sabina after I returned home from my three weeks at the police station.

"Do you want to go?" she asked.

"Not really," I answered. "But when the communists arrest people, they can keep them in jail for years. What if they arrest you, too? Who would take care of Mihai? He would be homeless. And he might start following communism instead of God."

A pastor friend came to our house. During his visit, he kept reminding us of the angel's words to Lot in Genesis.

"Escape for your life! Do not look behind you!" the angel said.

After our visitor left, I asked Sabina, "Don't you think that may have been a message from God to escape for our lives? Was it a warning that I should save my life by fleeing?"

"Escape for what life?" she answered.

Then she went to the bedroom and got her Bible. She brought it to me opened to Matthew 16:25.

"'Whoever desires to save his life will lose it,'" she read. "'But whoever loses his life for My sake will find it.' If we leave now, would you ever be able to preach about that verse again?"

> "Under cruel rulers, prison is the most honorable place to be."
>
> —Richard Wurmbrand

"We can't help the Christians in Romania if we are in jail," I said. "But we might be able to send them help if we go to another country."

"I think we have to stay, Richard," said Sabina.

■ ■ ■

We had started holding secret meetings around our city of Bucharest, in the homes of our Christian friends. Meeting in homes was safer than meeting in churches.

One night, about fifty of us gathered in the home of a friend. Our friend used to be a rich man. But the communists had taken away all his fine belongings. Soon they would take his house.

We took turns standing guard in case the police came. A secret prayer meeting like this could have landed us all in jail.

About midnight, one woman spoke up.

"You!" she said. "The one who is thinking of leaving! Remember, Jesus the good shepherd did not leave His flock. He stayed to the end."

At dawn when the meeting ended, Sabina and I walked home through cold streets. It was January, and snow was beginning to fall.

"We can't leave now," said Sabina.

I agreed. I believed God was speaking to me through the woman at the prayer meeting.

"We're here to stay," we later told our friends.

This news made them very happy.

Many years later, I saw the woman who had given the warning at the prayer meeting. She was waiting for me at the train station when I returned home from prison. She met me with flowers.

"Thank you for your advice," I said. "I'm not sorry I followed it."

Official Church

"Official churches" are churches allowed or supported by the government. Sometimes communist countries allow official Christian churches to exist.

Leaders of these churches must be approved by the government, and the government tells them what to do. If the government rules say, "You must not teach children," or "You must not preach from certain parts of the Bible," the official church leaders are expected to obey the government.

In countries where the government tries to control the church, usually fewer than 10 percent of the Christians attend official churches. The others would rather worship in underground churches and follow God's rules instead of the government's rules.

CHAPTER 7

Without a Trace!

Sabina Wurmbrand tells what happened in February after the January prayer meeting.

We lived close enough to the church to walk to Sunday services. On Sunday, February 29 ("**Leap Day**"), 1948, Richard left for church a little early.

"I want to get a few things done before church starts," my husband said.

"That's fine," I answered. "I'll meet you there in half an hour."

Soon I arrived at the church office. Pastor Solheim, Richard's helper, was there. But Richard wasn't.

> **Leap Day:** February 29th, called Leap Day because it happens only once every four years, during Leap Year.

"Richard hasn't turned up yet," he said. "Maybe he met a friend who needed help. He'll be here."

But he didn't come. Pastor Solheim preached in Richard's place. I phoned friends, but Richard wasn't with any of them. Fear grew in my heart.

Sunday lunch at our home was usually a happy, crowded celebration. Friends gathered to talk and sing. For many, this became the highlight of their week.

Friends came on February 29, too. But there was little talking and no singing. We sat silently, waiting for Richard. He never showed up. I smiled as I remembered the times before when he had come home late after helping someone in need.

Surely he must be doing something like that now, I thought.

That afternoon, Richard was supposed to perform a wedding for a young couple in the church. Pastor Solheim filled in for him.

Maybe he's sick or hurt, and someone drove him to the hospital, I thought.

I phoned all the hospitals. Then I went to their emergency rooms. But he wasn't at any of the hospitals.

I finally had to admit to myself that he probably had been arrested.

The next day I went to a government office called the **Ministry of the Interior**. I had

Ministry of the Interior:
A government department headed by a *minister*. In this case, a minister is a government official rather than the pastor of a church.

heard that important prisoners were kept in the Interior Ministry's basement.

When I got there, the stairs to the office were crowded with women and children looking for their husbands, sons, and fathers.

"Where is my husband?" the woman at the head of the line asked the officials. "He has been missing for days!"

She gave an official her husband's name. He pretended to look through long lists of names. He peered into filing cabinets.

"We don't know where he is," he lied. "Have you tried the hospitals?"

The officials claimed that no trace could be found of all those missing men. When I got to the front of the line, they told me the same story.

I went from office to office trying to find someone who would tell me where Richard was. Pastor Solheim came with me to the office of one official.

"I have information about Pastor Wurmbrand," she said to us. "My information is that he was seen sneaking out of the country with a suitcase full of the church's money. He told church members that the money would be used to help the poor. But instead, he stole it! Now he is in Denmark."

The official's story was ridiculous. No one believed it.

Night after night, I sat looking out the window.

He'll come home tonight, I thought. *He's done nothing wrong. They'll let him go.*

But he didn't come. I put my forehead against the windowpane and sighed.

We had prayed that God would allow us to bear a cross. But would we be strong enough to bear it?

■ ■ ■

Pastor Wurmbrand tells his story of February 29.

As I walked to church that morning, a black van stopped in front of me. Four men got out. They surrounded me and pushed me into the van.

It wasn't the first time I had been arrested. So I knew my "kidnappers" were the communist secret police. They drove me through the city streets to their headquarters.

Inside the building, they took away my identification papers and other belongings. They even took my tie and shoelaces. Finally, they took away my name.

"From now on," said the official on duty, "your name is Vasile Georgescu."

It was a common Romanian name. This way, even the prison guards would not know my real name.

If anyone asked them, "Is Richard Wurmbrand in your prison?" they would say, "No."

Richard Wurmbrand, like so many other Romanians, would disappear without a trace.

Without a Trace!

They took me to an empty cell. There was a small window high in the concrete wall of the cell, and two beds made of wooden planks. I sat on one of the beds and waited for the police to come get me for questioning.

During peacetime, soldiers prepare for war. Like them, I had prepared myself—but I prepared for prison. I had studied the lives of Christians who suffered because they refused to deny Christ.

I decided that I would not reveal the names of any friends who had helped me spread the gospel. With God's help, I would betray no one when questioned.

Will my faith be strong enough to stand up to the test? I wondered.

Then I remembered that the Bible says, "Do not be afraid" 366 times. That's one time for all 365 days of the year—plus one more for the extra day in Leap Year. God had not forgotten today, February 29, Leap Day!

God was with me. I did not need to be afraid. What an amazing discovery!

Struggles and hardships lay ahead. But I would also make many more wonderful discoveries. First, though, I needed to try to figure out a way to let Sabina know where I was.

PART TWO

Imprisoned for Christ

CHAPTER 8

Hard Times

Again I was expelled from school!

My teacher was a communist.

"The Bible is not true," he said to the class. "Science gives us the answers to all of life's questions."

Then he told us to write an essay. In the essay, we were to tell why the Bible is false.

"The Bible is true," I wrote. "Arguments against the Bible are weak. Surely the teacher has not read the Bible. The Bible is in harmony with true science."

It was not the first time I had been expelled. It would not be the last.

After I was expelled, I would stay out of school for a time. Then I would enroll in a different school.

After a while, being expelled meant nothing to me. I did not fear it. As a Christian, I would never be able to get a good job anyway as long as the communists were in

power. So I felt a great freedom to tell the truth. I had
nothing to hang on to but my faith.

■ ■ ■

Sometimes when I told the truth, it encouraged others
who felt afraid. One day, a teacher gave a speech about
atheism to my class. He wanted to prove that there is no
God.

I stood up.

"Teaching is a big responsibility," I said as politely as I
could manage. "The Bible tells us that not many people
should become teachers, because they will be judged more
strictly.

"By teaching that there is no God, you may have led
many young people astray today. According to Jesus, it
would be better for a man to be thrown into the sea with a
big stone around his neck than for him to lead believers
astray."

One by one, other students rose up and agreed with
me. Soon the whole class stood together. They just needed
someone with courage to speak up first.

I guess the school officials didn't want to expel the
whole class, because we weren't punished that day.

■ ■ ■

"Mother, I'm through with school," I said when I got home
from another school one day.

"What do you mean, 'through'?" she asked.

"I'm not going back."

"But you need to try to finish your studies!" she said.

"Not at *that* school, I don't! Today the teacher asked us to choose someone to receive a reward. The class elected me."

"That's wonderful, Mihai!" said Mother.

"The reward was the red necktie that is worn by the members of the Communist Youth Club," I explained.

"Oh, I see," she said, beginning to understand.

"I refused to wear it. I told the teacher, 'I won't wear the tie of the Party that puts Christians in prison.'"

"Then what happened?" Mother asked, fearing the worst.

"The teacher is Jewish," I said. "I know she doesn't like the communists. But I think she is afraid of what they might do to her if she disagrees with them. She scolded me in front of everyone and sent me home. And I'm not going back!"

But I did go back. Mother took me to school the next day and talked to the teacher. The teacher hugged me and welcomed me back. She and some of the other teachers often tried to protect me.

Time after time I stood up and argued with instructors. Sometimes I lost the arguments, because they could argue better than I could. But I stood up for the truth anyway.

The teachers who weren't communists were kind to me. They liked my courage.

Mother said, "Romania is not a communist country. It is a country held captive by the communists."

She knew that many Romanians hated communism. But they were afraid to speak up.

If they said anything against communism, they might end up in prison like my father. Then their children would be expelled from school just because their mother or father was a Christian prisoner.

I was expelled not only for standing up for the truth myself. I was also expelled more than once because my father was in prison for standing up for the truth.

Even though the government tried to hide that they had arrested my father, we discovered the truth. But finding the proof wasn't easy.

■ ■ ■

Mother went to the offices of many government officials. But no one would tell her where my father was. Many other people in Romania had the same problem.

One day, a neighbor came to visit.

"Have you heard of a government official named Theohari?" the neighbor asked. "His brother lives down the street. I've heard that the brother will get people out of prison. I can talk to him for you."

The official's brother agreed to help us if we promised to tell no one.

"If you pay me, I will convince my brother to get Pastor Wurmbrand out of jail," he said. "You have my word."

Hard Times

He asked for more money than we had. It wasn't easy, but we got it. We handed the money over to Theohari's brother.

Nothing happened. We had been cheated.

Others tried to trick us in the same way. We wasted months listening to the false promises of people who couldn't really help us.

■ ■ ■

One evening, a stranger came to the door.

"I've seen your husband," he told my mother. "I'm a prison guard. I take him his food. I will tell you more if you pay me."

We were doubtful.

"How do I know you're telling the truth?" Mother asked. "Maybe if you bring me a few words written in Richard's handwriting, I will believe you."

She gave him a chocolate candy bar.

"Take this to Richard and bring back a message with his signature on the wrapper," she said.

Two days later, the man came back. He took off his hat. Then he pulled the candy bar wrapper out of a hidden pocket in the hat's lining.

"My dearest wife, I thank you for your sweetness. I am well. Love, Richard," the words on the wrapper said.

It was my father's handwriting! Finally we knew he was alive and well. We paid the prison guard, and he continued to secretly deliver messages from time to time.

Imprisoned for Christ

■ ■ ■

It didn't make sense. Some government officials wouldn't admit that my father was a prisoner. Others persecuted us because he was.

The government refused to give my mother a **ration card**. Why? Because she was the wife of a Christian prisoner.

A ration card was necessary to get food. Without a ration card, you couldn't get even a loaf of bread legally.

Only workers could get ration cards. Only people acceptable to the government could be workers. Wives of Christian prisoners were not acceptable to the government.

"How am I to live? How can I feed my son?" Mother asked the officials.

"That's your problem," they answered.

For a while, we raised silk-worms to earn money. I wasn't enthusiastic about having worms sharing our tiny apartment. But I gathered mulberry leaves from trees in a nearby cemetery to feed them. When they turned into cocoons, we sold them to silk makers. We earned enough money to buy a little food.

> **Ration Card:** A card that allows a person or family to receive *rations*. A ration is an amount of food or other provisions. Rations are sometimes used to control how much food people get during times when food is scarce.

Then one batch of worms got sick. I whistled a funeral march on my way to the library to check out a book about silkworms. The book said the worms would not recover. So we gave up on raising them. I didn't miss them.

Hard Times

Mother also sewed and knitted to get food money. Later I learned how to repair musical instruments. Sometimes friends brought us food.

■ ■ ■

I found ways to keep up my studies while I was expelled from school. So by the age of fifteen, I was ready to take the exams that would allow me to graduate from high school.

I failed the written test. One of the questions asked me to compare religion and communism and to show that religion was old-fashioned.

Instead, I explained that the Bible revealed scientific truths long before the communists were born.

"God's Word tells us in Isaiah 40:22 that the earth is a sphere," I wrote. "Job 26:7 says correctly that the world hangs on nothing."

I continued praising the wisdom of the Bible.

I had to appear before a professor for the oral part of the exam. He had read my answers to the written questions, and he knew I had failed.

"What made you risk your whole future by writing an answer like that?" the professor asked.

The Bible advises us to always be ready to give an answer about our faith. With God's help, I was ready.

"Nothing you are hanging onto will help you on Judgment Day," I said to him. "On that day, it won't matter how much science you know. And you cannot be saved by calling out 'Marx, Marx.' The Bible says only those who call on the name of the Lord will be saved."

I talked with the professor for two hours. I even invited him to a house church meeting.

He gave me a low grade, but it was a passing grade.

"You are lucky you got me as your professor," he told me.

I was glad I passed. But I was even happier when the professor came to church and gave his life to Jesus!

■ ■ ■

I wanted to go to college because I love to learn. New languages are especially fun to study. Besides Romanian, I learned how to speak German, French, Italian, and Portuguese. And I learned to read Spanish, Chinese, Hebrew, and Greek.

But I never learned Russian, the language of the communist invaders. They forced us to study it in school two hours a day, three days a week, for twelve years. I studied it, but I couldn't remember it.

Maybe I didn't like being forced to learn something I didn't want to learn. All I ever really remembered about Russian was the alphabet.

■ ■ ■

Life in college was not any easier. After I was expelled the third time, I managed to enroll again. But then some communist officials visited me.

"Wouldn't you like to finish college and get a good job?" one of them asked.

Yes, I would like that, I thought. *But I probably won't like your idea of how I can do it.*

"You can stay in school if you will just agree to one thing. Report to us once a week about your fellow students. Tell us which students are Christians. Let us know which ones say bad things about the government or about communism. That's all you have to do."

I thought about it. It would be nice to finally finish school. The government would find out what the other students were doing even if I didn't tell them. Surely I had suffered enough over the years! Would it really be so bad to cooperate with the communists, just this once?

It was a big test of my faith. God helped me pass the test. I refused to report on the other students. Again I was expelled.

■ ■ ■

My mother and I suffered daily because we were living for Christ in enemy territory. But as hard as it was for us on the outside, my father was having much worse struggles in prison.

CHAPTER 9

Alone with God

I was questioned many times when I first arrived at the prison. The guards came to my cell and blindfolded me so I couldn't see. They led me down a hall to a room where they sat me in a chair. Then they took off the blindfold.

At my first questioning, the guards gave me a pen and some paper.

"Write about your life," one guard demanded. "Confess your crimes."

I pulled my chair closer to a desk in the room and began writing. But I didn't confess any "crimes," because I hadn't committed any. Instead, I wrote an outline of my life up to the time when I became a Christian.

Then I thought, *Communist officials might read what I am writing. I will write about how I used to be an atheist like they are. Then I will explain how the eyes of an atheist can be opened to the truth.*

I hoped to lead a communist to Christ by doing this.

After about an hour of writing, a guard led me back to my cell. During the next few weeks, I was taken to different officials for more questioning.

Sometimes, the officials asked me to write lists of names.

"Write down the names of everyone you know," one questioner ordered.

"Make a list of all the people to whom you have told secrets," another demanded.

They were pleased when I gave them long lists of names. They hoped the lists would lead them to more Christians to arrest.

But God helped me never to say or write anything that would bring harm to another person. Sometimes I gave the officials the names of people who had died. Once I listed only communists working for the government. Another time I wrote down the names of people who had fled Romania to live in other countries.

The questioners were angry after they checked the names.

"Don't you know that I can order someone to shoot you right now?" shouted one official.

"Officer," I answered calmly, "you have an opportunity to do an experiment. You say that you can have me killed. I know you are telling the truth about that. So put your hand on my chest. If my heart is beating fast, that means I am afraid of death. Then you can know that there is no God and no eternal life. But if my heart is beating calmly, then you must think again. There is a God; there is eternal life."

"You fool!" bellowed the officer. "Your Savior, or whatever you call Him, is not going to get you out of this prison!"

"His name is Jesus, and if He wishes, He can release me," I said.

■ ■ ■

But God had more for me to learn before He released me. After I spent seven months in one prison, officials transferred me to a cell in the basement of the Ministry of the Interior building.

For the next two years, I lived in solitary confinement —*very* solitary confinement. I had no cellmates, nothing to read, and no writing materials. I had only my thoughts to keep me company.

During this time, I heard almost no noise. The guards even wore shoes with soft soles so the prisoners could not hear them walking.

Everything was dull, colorless, and boring. I never saw the sun, moon, or stars. Flowers and snow were just a memory.

■ ■ ■

I noticed the prison guard peering at me through the spy hole in my cell door. What he saw must have amazed him.

I jumped and sprang all around my solitary cell. It wasn't easy. The cell was very small. When I paced, I could take only three paces in each direction before I ran into the wall.

But now I leaped.

The guard's eye disappeared from the spy hole.

When he returned, he brought some food from the guards' kitchen. He gave me a loaf of bread, cheese, and some sugar. That was more food than a prisoner ate during an entire week! What a reward!

Maybe the guard had orders to be sure that the prisoners did not get out of control. I didn't try to explain my actions to the guard, but I was not out of control.

The Book of Luke tells us that Jesus said, "Blessed are you when men hate you, when they exclude you and insult you and reject your name as evil, because of the Son of Man. Rejoice in that day and leap for joy, because great is your reward..."

I had learned to enjoy the presence of God in my cell.

But one day, I thought to myself, *I've carried out only half the command. I've rejoiced, but that is not enough. Jesus said that we must also leap.*

So I leaped. And great *was* my reward when the guard discovered me leaping!

■ ■ ■

Alone with God

Even in solitary confinement, I kept busy. Sometimes the days were not long enough for all that I had to do!

I started every day with prayer. In my prayer, I traveled through the whole world, praying for every country and town I could remember. I prayed for pilots, sea captains, and those in prisons. Then I prayed for my family, my friends, and my persecutors.

Since I had no Bible, I read the Bible from memory. I was thankful for the Scriptures I had memorized.

I made two sets of chessmen out of pieces of bread, and I played chess with myself. In two years, I never lost a game! I always won with one set of pieces or the other.

Every day I composed a sermon and preached it. In 1 Peter 1:12, the Bible says that angels want to look into the preaching of the gospel. So I supposed that unseen angels listened to my sermons.

In my sermons, I often told stories like this one:

A young king liked to start trouble. He gave no peace to the wise old king who lived in a nearby country.

The old king tried to have peaceful relations with the young king's nation. But it was not to be. The young king started a war.

The old king remembered that he himself had not been wise when he was young. So he gave orders to his officers to capture the young king, but not to hurt him.

The young king was soon captured and brought in chains to the old king. The old king felt sorry for his captive. But he pretended to be angry with him.

"I will give you one chance to get free," the old king said. "Tomorrow I will give you a jug of water, full to the brim. You must carry it from one end of our main street to the other without spilling a drop. If you fail, I will throw you in prison. If you succeed, I will let you go."

The next day the procession started. First came the young king with the jug of water. Guards surrounded him so he wouldn't try to escape. The jailer followed him.

The old king had ordered his subjects to stand along both sides of the street. The people on one side of the street were commanded to boo and mock the prisoner. Those on the other side were told to cheer and encourage him.

The young king succeeded. He didn't spill a drop.

The old king asked him, "When so many people were mocking you, why didn't you answer them?"

The young man replied, "I had no time for that. I had to be careful about my water jug."

"Did you thank the ones who cheered and encouraged you?" asked the king.

"No," the young king answered. "Their praise couldn't help me. I had to pay attention to my jug."

The old king set the young one free with this advice: "You have been given a soul. You have to bring it back to the Lord whole and clean. That is the only thing that matters. Don't seek the praise of men by picking fights so you can win cheap victories. Don't worry if people mock you. Pay attention only to your walk with God."

Alone with God

After I preached a sermon, I made up a poem that summarized the lesson of the sermon. Then I memorized the poem.

When I got out of prison, I wrote down these sermons. I later published them in books.

■ ■ ■

Tap. Tap. Tap.

One day I heard a faint tapping on the cell wall beside my bed.

What could it mean? I wondered.

Tap. Tap. Tap. The noise continued.

I tapped back. Suddenly I heard a flurry of taps by my bed.

Someone must be signaling me, I thought.

After a while, I realized that the prisoner in the next cell was trying to teach me a simple code.

A = 1 tap
B = 2 taps
C = 3 taps
And so on.

"Who are you?" was the first message my neighbor sent.

"A pastor," I replied.

It took a long time to send a message. We improved the code so it would not take so long. In the new code, one tap stood for the first five letters of the alphabet, two taps for the second group of five, and so on. A second tap told whether the letter was the first, second, third, fourth, or fifth letter in its group. So "B" was a single tap, followed by a pause, then two more taps.

> A = 1 tap, pause, 1 tap
> B = 1 tap, pause, 2 taps
> C = 1 tap, pause, 3 taps
> D = 1 tap, pause, 4 taps
> E = 1 tap, pause, 5 taps
> F = 2 taps, pause, 1 tap
> G = 2 taps, pause, 2 taps
> And so on.

Then my neighbor, who had been a radio engineer, used this code to teach me Morse code. After that, we used Morse code to tell jokes, to pass along news, and even to communicate chess moves.

I taught my prisoners Bible verses and shared the gospel with unbelievers. Soon I left solitary confinement and joined other prisoners who needed to learn about Jesus.

Not that leaving solitary confinement was a happy occasion. I was transferred to another prison, but not for joyful reasons. And I did not go to a better place.

CHAPTER 10

Room Four

I had been sent to a prison hospital because I had TB—**tuberculosis**.

Prisoners were still wearing what they had on when they were arrested. Week after week, month after month, we wore the same clothes. Hardly anything was provided for us and little was done to help us—even when we were sick.

When I first got to the hospital, a doctor examined me.

"I won't lie to you," he said. "There's nothing we can do. You may have only two weeks to live. Try to eat what they give you."

As I waited for my food, I listened while the doctor examined another prisoner.

"I'm feeling better today," the prisoner lied. "Really I am! Please, please don't let them take me to Room Four."

Tuberculosis: A serious lung disease that causes coughing, fever, weight loss, and chest pain.

"What happens in Room Four?" I asked the man who brought my food.

"It's known as the 'Death Room.' That's where you go when they know there is no hope that you will get well," he told me.

I tried to eat the soup he brought, but could not. Someone fed me with a spoon. I threw up.

"I'm sorry," said the doctor. "You'll have to go to Room Four."

The doctor looked at me with pity. He was a Christian prisoner, too. Since there was a shortage of doctors, the guards let him examine people.

But there was nothing he could do to help me.

"If only we had some good medicine in here," he said sadly.

■ ■ ■

I was extremely sick. Eleven other prisoners lived in Room Four, and they were all very sick, too. But not as sick as I was.

I couldn't even turn over in my bed. So the other prisoners helped me. They gave me water and tried to make me comfortable.

After a few days, the doctor's look of pity changed to puzzlement. He said he was surprised that I hadn't died yet. My fever fell slightly, and my mind was clearer.

I began to listen to the other prisoners talking. Their conversations were different from those of prisoners outside of Room Four. These prisoners—the sickest of the sick—didn't brag or argue. They expected to die soon, and they didn't want to waste time with such foolishness.

I stayed in Room Four for thirty months. During that time, I saw many men die.

Not one of them died an atheist.

Communists, thieves, rich men, and poor peasants were locked together in one small cell. Yet none of them died without making peace with God. Their atheism broke down in the face of death.

■ ■ ■

Sometimes prisoners from other parts of the hospital came to Room Four. They helped care for us and offered us comfort.

One day, at Easter time, a prisoner brought a small piece of paper with something wrapped inside. He gave it to his sick friend, a man named Gafencu.

"Open it!" he said. "Someone smuggled it into the hospital."

Gafencu unwrapped the paper. There were two lumps of sugar in it! He stared at it, amazed.

None of us had seen sugar for years. We longed for the taste of something sweet.

Everyone stared at Gafencu and the treasure in his hands. What would he do with it?

He wrapped it up again.

"I won't eat it," he said. "Someone might be sicker than I am. I will save it to give to him."

He put the gift beside his bed.

A few days later, my fever rose and I became very weak. The sugar was passed from bed to bed until it came to rest on mine.

"It's a present for you," said Gafencu.

"Thank you," I said.

I knew the sugar would taste wonderfully delicious. But what if someone needed it more than I did? I saved it.

When I felt better, I gave it to a former thief named Soteris.

Soteris used to brag about being an atheist and about all he had stolen. After he got sick, he cried out to God for help. And he never stole the sugar, though it would have been easy to do so. Instead, when it came to him, he too saved it for someone who was sicker.

For two years, the sugar passed from man to man. Twice it returned to me. When I left Room Four, it was still there.

■ ■ ■

A musician named Avram joined us in the Death Room. He could hum long passages of music composed by classical musicians. For hours at a time, he entertained us by humming Bach, Beethoven, and Mozart—our own personal concert.

But Avram brought a more precious gift with him. Because of an injury to his spine, he wore a plaster body cast. We watched as he slipped his hand inside the turtle-like shell and took out a tattered book.

"A book!" I exclaimed. I hadn't seen a book in several years. "What is it? Where did you get it?"

"It's the Gospel of John," said Avram. "I hid it in my cast when the police came for me. Would you like to borrow it?"

I held the book in my hands as carefully as if it were a baby bird. No life-saving medicine could have been more precious to me.

Before I went to prison, I had memorized many Scripture verses. But I forgot more and more of them each day without a Bible.

Now several prisoners would learn the Book of John by heart while I re-learned it. We discussed it every day. Avram's smuggled Gospel helped bring many prisoners to Christ.

We had to be careful and keep this secret from some of the prisoners. If someone told the guards about the book, it would be taken away.

■　■　■

After many months in Room Four, I finally felt well enough to get out of bed each day. At first, I took just a few steps and returned to bed.

Two doctors came to examine me.

"We don't understand," said one of the doctors. "You've had no medicine. You should be dead."

"If I have recovered, it is a miracle of God and an answer to prayer," I told them.

"Well, you're really no better," said the other doctor. "But you're no worse either. We're going to move you out of Room Four."

My friends there were very happy. My leaving the room gave them hope. Until now, no one had left Room Four alive.

I knew that many prisoners had prayed for me to get well. My family prayed, too, as did members of my congregation in Bucharest.

But not for many years did I learn about the thousands of people around the world who had joined in the prayers of my family and friends.

■ ■ ■

I didn't forget the prisoners I left behind.

The guards at the hospital decided to let us receive one package a month from home. I wrote and asked if someone would please send food and "Dr. Filon's old clothes."

The request for Dr. Filon's clothes puzzled my family. The doctor was a small man. I was very tall. I hoped they would guess that what I really wanted was some medicine from Dr. Filon. We were not allowed to ask for medicine in our packages.

In my next month's package, a small packet of TB medicine lay hidden among the food and clothes!

"Who is the sickest person in Room Four?" I asked Stavrat, a friend of mine. "Whoever it is, I want to give him the medicine."

"Sultaniuc is very sick," said Stavrat. "But he's very rude and cranky. I don't like him. Why don't you take the medicine yourself?"

I insisted, so Stavrat agreed to go tell Sultaniuc about the medicine. Soon he came back.

"Sultaniuc wanted to know where the medicine came from," Stavrat reported. "I told him it came from you. He said if it was yours, he doesn't want it. He used to be an Iron Guard terrorist, and he said you are no friend of the Iron Guard. I told you he is rude."

I asked Josif, another prisoner, to carry the medicine to Sultaniuc. "The medicine is not mine—it's God's," I explained. "I gave it to Him the moment it arrived. So tell Sultaniuc it is not from me."

Sultaniuc took the medicine from Josif.

It was one of many opportunities I had to demonstrate the love of Christ.

The communists did not love those who mistreated them. Often, they were mean, even to people who agreed with them.

Prisoners who saw Christians living out the gospel came closer and closer to the faith every day. But not everyone in the prison wanted Christians in their midst.

CHAPTER 11

A Captive Audience

For a pastor, prison is just a new place to preach. At church on Sunday in the free world, the pastor may ring a bell. People hear the bell, and if they wish, they come to church. If not, they don't come.

If a man does not like the pastor's sermon one Sunday, the next Sunday he stays home. If it rains he might stay home, even if he liked the sermon.

Church members in free countries look at their watches.

"He has already preached for thirty minutes!" they say. "Will he never quit?"

But when prisoners are arrested, their watches are taken away from them.

As a pastor in a prison, I had my "congregation" with me seven days a week. I could preach to them from morning to night! Some listened eagerly—but others weren't as enthusiastic.

"Stop!" cried a prisoner named Lazar one day as I preached to a group. "No more about Christianity, please! Don't you know there are other interesting religions?"

"Well," I said, "I know a few things about Buddhism and Confucianism. Let me tell you a story."

I then told him a story from the New Testament. But I didn't tell him where the story came from. He thought it was from the teachings of another religion.

"Fascinating!" Lazar exclaimed. "That is a beautiful story!"

"I'm glad you think so," I said. "It is actually a story from the Bible. Why do you run after other religions? Is it a case of 'the grass is always greener on the other side of the fence'? You should study the Bible more. Jesus will provide everything you will ever need."

■ ■ ■

I was moved to a prison that held hardened criminals. The criminals loved to argue. They got angry over the least little things.

When I tried to preach to them, they groaned or pretended to snore. After a sermon, they began discussing what I had said. Their discussion turned into quarrels.

I had to do something different. I discovered that they listened to stories, especially stories about crime.

A Captive Audience

One of the stories I told went like this:

Long ago there were two brothers. The older was good and holy. The younger brother often got into trouble and liked to hang around with friends who were even worse than he was.

The older brother prayed for the younger. He often pleaded with him to change his life and to go to church. But it seemed useless. The younger brother would not change.

One evening, the older brother sat in his room reading. Suddenly the younger brother rushed into the room.

"Help me!" he begged. "The police are after me! I robbed a jewelry store!"

The younger brother had run through the woods and a muddy field to avoid the police. His clothes were torn and dirty. Watches, rings, and bracelets were hanging from his bulging pockets.

"I'll help you," said the older brother. "Quickly, change clothes with me!"

He put on the dirty clothes of the criminal and gave his white shirt and clean pants to his brother. They had barely finished exchanging clothes when the police arrived.

Seeing the older brother in dirty clothes full of jewelry, they arrested him. Brought before a judge, the older brother pleaded guilty.

"I take responsibility for the crime," he said.

The judge sentenced him to jail.

"Have you anything you'd like to say?" he asked the innocent brother.

"Only one thing," said the older brother. "I want to send my brother this letter I have written."

His wish was granted. The next day the younger brother got the letter.

"Dear Brother," it said. "At this moment, I am in jail in your place, for your crime, wearing your clothes. I am happy to offer this sacrifice for you.

"But I would like to ask you something. As you wear the clean clothes I gave you, lead a life of goodness and purity. I ask nothing else."

On reading those words, the younger brother felt ashamed of his deeds. He ran to the judge to confess his crime. But the judge would not listen to him.

"A crime was committed. It is paid for. What happened between you and your brother is none of my business," said the judge.

The younger brother continued to live in undeserved freedom. One day his old friends visited him.

"Come join us," they urged. "It will be fun. We'll do the things we used to do."

"No," the younger brother would answer. "I can't do evil deeds in the clean clothes given to me by my innocent brother, who is paying for my crime."

Some of the criminals understood that my story was really about Jesus. They were reminded that Someone cared for them and paid for their sins even though He was sinless.

Other prisoners just thought it was a strange story. They had heard a Christian message without knowing it.

A Captive Audience

■ ■ ■

I was transferred to a cell that was already miserably full. The bunks and the floor were packed with prisoners. No one could move without bumping against someone else. The last thing the men wanted was another cellmate.

The guard pushed me in and banged the door shut. I told the prisoners I was a pastor, and said a short prayer. They cursed me.

Then, in the dim light, someone called my name from an upper bunk.

"Pastor Wurmbrand," he called. "I recognize your voice! I heard your speech at the meeting of religious leaders held by the communists many years ago. Do you remember the speech?"

"Yes, of course," I answered. "I'm quite sure that speech is one of the reasons I'm here today. But—who are you?"

"We'll talk tomorrow," he replied.

It was a long night. Anyone who turned over in his sleep woke his neighbor. Wakened prisoners cursed and woke up everyone else.

At 5 a.m., a guard struck a dangling piece of railroad tracks with an iron bar.

Clang!

That was our alarm clock.

The man from the upper bunk climbed down to shake my hand. He had a piece of cloth tied around his head.

"It's good I knew your voice," he said when he got close enough to see me. "I wouldn't have recognized you by sight.

How thin you are! By looking at you I can tell the communists have gotten their revenge for your speech.

"Let me introduce myself," he continued. "My name is Nassim."

"It's a pleasure to meet you, Nassim."

Nassim was a Muslim leader. The cloth around his head was a symbol of his religion, Islam.

Our friendship began at the next meal. The guards brought us something they called soup. But it was more like pieces of rotten cabbage floating in scum. I drank it all.

"How can you eat that horrible stuff?" Nassim asked in amazement.

"It's a Christian secret," I answered. "I think of the apostle Paul's words, 'Rejoice with those who rejoice.' In America right now there are people who are eating fried chicken. I thank God with them as I take the first drink of soup. Next I rejoice with friends in England who are eating roast beef. Then I drink another mouthful. So, by thinking of friends in many countries, I rejoice with those who rejoice. And I stay alive."

Nassim and I had to share a bunk through the hot, stuffy nights. I was thankful not to be on the floor.

Everyone around us tossed and turned.

"You lie very still," said Nassim. "What are you thinking? Does the apostle Paul help you now, too?"

I replied, "Yes, now I rejoice with those in comfortable homes in free countries. I think about their books, vacations, music, and children. I also remember the second part of what Paul said: 'Weep with those who weep.' I thank God for those around the world who weep and pray for us."

I felt blessed to be able to share words from the Bible with a Muslim.

■ ■ ■

Prisoners came and went. Each time men left, others took their place, and I got new members for my "congregation."

I met two new men. One used to be an Iron Guard leader. He was in prison serving a twenty-year sentence. The other was a thief who had stolen small items. The thief had served six months and was due to be freed soon.

"I know how to get out of here," the Iron Guard leader whispered to me.

Then he went over to the thief.

"You know," he told the thief, "the government has agreed to free all former Iron Guard members next month. I'm going to be one of the first to leave."

"Is that so?" asked the thief, who believed the man. "Well, I'm getting out soon, too. All I want is a good job. But no one will give me one."

"I'm so sorry," said the Iron Guard man. Suddenly he grabbed the thief's arm. "I've got an idea!" he said, continuing his story. "I have important friends on the outside. They are going to help run the government soon. But it will be a few weeks before they are in power. So why don't we switch names? At the next roll call, you answer to my name and I'll answer to yours. As soon as they let me go in your place, I'll start talking to my friends about a job for you. Then when you get out in a month—with my name—my friends will be in power. You can have a job and a great future!"

The thief agreed. He started using the Iron Guard leader's name.

Ten days later, the Iron Guard man—using the thief's name—was released. Months went by and the thief still was not free. He had been tricked! So he reported the matter to prison officials.

The officials hunted down the Iron Guard member and brought him back to prison.

"Now I'll be free!" said the thief.

But he wasn't freed. Instead, he was charged with helping a prisoner escape. He got a twenty-year sentence of his own!

The two men had to go on living together in prison. They, like others in the prison, needed to learn how to treat others fairly and forgive those who wronged them.

■ ■ ■

Soon there was another opportunity to preach about love and kindness. But this sermon was preached with actions, not words.

Boots were a luxury in prison. Some men had no shoes at all. Their feet froze in the unheated cells.

A Captive Audience

Once a day, the guards let us go outside for exercise in the small prison yard. During the winter, those without shoes stayed inside.

My Christian friend Stavrat was blessed to own a warm pair of boots. One day, he gave them away to a man who had no shoes. The man who received the boots learned much about Christian love. No sermon could have taught him more.

I preached the second sermon in this wordless sermon series. Stavrat and I shared my boots. Every other day, Stavrat wore the boots outside for exercise while I stayed inside. On the remaining days, I wore the boots as he stayed inside.

■ ■ ■

Some men sacrificed more than boots.

The prison grew so crowded that the guards often did not know all the prisoners by name. That's how the Iron Guard leader and the thief could trade names.

When the guards wanted to punish someone, they came to the cell and called out a prisoner's name. Then they took the prisoner to another room.

It is sad how cruel men without Christ can behave. Sometimes the guards beat the prisoners with whips. I myself was beaten at times. God gave me the strength to endure it. He even helped me to love and pray for my persecutors.

Imprisoned for Christ

A pastor in the prison, Pastor Milon, became a great hero of the Christian faith. Often when the guards called out the name of another prisoner, Pastor Milon answered. He took a beating for someone else.

The prisoners respected Pastor Milon. They also learned to respect Jesus, in whose name Pastor Milon sacrificed himself.

■ ■ ■

One afternoon, we ate rotten carrot soup for lunch.

I sat on a neighbor's bunk to eat with him. If I had someone to talk to, it was easier to forget the taste of prison food.

My neighbor told me that he used to be a radio engineer. On his radio, he had sent messages to someone in another country about things that were happening in Romania. Government officials caught him, and he was sent to prison.

"I used Morse code in my work, of course," he said. "And it was my knowledge of Morse code that brought me to Christ."

"Oh, really?"

"Yes, it happened five or six years ago. I was in a cell at the Ministry of the Interior building. A pastor was in the next cell. The pastor tapped Bible verses to me through the wall."

When he told me his cell number, I said, "I was that pastor."

A Captive Audience

We had a joyful reunion, praising God for His goodness.

■ ■ ■

For a while in prison, I was pastor to no one. Instead, I needed a pastor myself.

It happened after a friend of mine named Popp took me aside one day. He had talked with men who came to our prison from other prisons.

"I'm afraid I have some bad news," he said. "Sabina is in prison. She has been sick, but she will live. She knows you are safe."

I couldn't stand the thought of my wife suffering the same kinds of things I suffered. And Mihai! Who was taking care of him?

I tried to pray, but a black gloom settled on my mind. For days I spoke to no one.

Then one morning in the prison yard, I saw an older pastor with a kind face.

Maybe he can help me, I thought.

I went to talk to him.

The pastor had more reason to mourn than I did. His daughter and son were in prison. Another son did not follow Christ. His grandchildren had been expelled from school.

But the pastor didn't seem gloomy like me. He spent his days cheering up others.

Instead of saying, "Good morning," he greeted everyone by saying, "Rejoice!"

"How can you rejoice after all your suffering?" I asked.

"There's always a reason to rejoice," he replied. "There's a God in heaven and in my heart. I had something to eat this morning. And look—the sun is shining! Many people love me. Every day that you do not rejoice is a day lost, Richard. You will never have that day again."

I, too, began to rejoice. But I didn't forget about Sabina.

CHAPTER 12

Sabina Imprisoned

Many women in our underground church had husbands in jail. We wanted to continue the work of the Lord in their absence.

Often we pretended to be nurses or maids. In such disguises, we visited families in our fellowship. We encouraged them and helped those who were struggling.

One night, I helped a man while he visited his wife in the hospital. I cleaned his house and took care of his six children until 11 p.m. Mihai spent that night with other friends.

When I finished, I was so tired! I planned to hurry home and go straight to bed.

But when I got home, I found my cousin very alarmed. He, his mother, and a Christian friend were visiting at my apartment.

"A suspicious man came while you were gone," said my cousin. "He said he came from the Living Space Office. He asked how many people live here. But I think he was really checking how many exits you have."

I knew then what to expect: a police raid. But I was almost too tired to worry. Mihai was safe at a friend's house. That was what mattered. I went to sleep, leaving Richard, Mihai, and all my loved ones in God's care.

At 5 a.m., the police pounded on the door. My cousin answered it. I heard shouting and boots clattering on the stairs up to my bedroom.

Six officers shoved their way into the small room.

"Sabina Wurmbrand!" shouted the man in charge. He never stopped shouting the whole time. "We know you're hiding weapons here! Show us where they are—*now!*"

Of course I had no guns.

The police opened closets and emptied drawers on the floor. A shelf of books crashed down. The men trampled over everything, yelling at us.

"So you won't tell us where the weapons are hidden? We'll tear this place apart!"

I picked up a Bible from under their feet.

"The only weapon we have in the house is here," I said, holding up the Bible.

The highest officer bellowed, "You're coming with us to make a full statement about your weapons!"

I laid the Bible on a table and said, "Please allow us a few minutes to pray. Then I'll go with you."

Sabina Imprisoned

They stood, astonished, as my friend and I prayed together. Then I hugged my cousin and his mother and left with the officers.

■　■　■

Years later, after Richard and I got out of prison, we compared stories. I had many of the same experiences he had. I had been questioned and asked to write down information about my life. I was also placed in solitary confinement for a time.

And like Richard, I endured life in overcrowded cells.

One such cell was in a prison called Jilava. Cell Four had space for thirty people. By Christmas in 1950, there were eighty people crammed into it. No one could move without treading on bodies lying in the aisles between the bunks.

One morning, we were overjoyed to be taken out for a shower—a rare treat. It had been a very long time since any of us had showered.

We stood to form a line. Some of the women had lain on their backs for months, and the exercise was too much for them. They fainted. Outside the cell, the guards pushed and shoved us along dark hallways.

As we hurried along, suddenly a woman turned around and screeched at the prisoner behind her, "You stepped on my sore heel!"

"I'm sorry," murmured the offender, a frail seventy-year-old named Mrs. Mihalache.

"Don't you know who I am?" the screechy woman hollered.

We all knew who she was—the worst informer in the cell. She spied on other inmates to get special favors from the guards.

"My dear," replied Mrs. Mihalache, "I scarcely know who I am anymore. How could I know who you are?"

The screechy informer shrieked even louder. The head guard blew his whistle.

"No showers!" he shouted. "Back to your cell! Move it!"

The guards shoved us back into Cell Four. The women began arguing. Some wanted revenge on the informer. Others wanted to punish the older woman.

The truth came out later. The showers didn't even work. The plumbing had broken down. An order had come from high government officials: Bathe the prisoners!

Some officials had visited Cell Four before the showers were ordered. One held a handkerchief over his nose because he thought we smelled bad. Maybe that was the reason for the order.

How could they wash so many women with no working showers? The head guard solved the problem. He arranged for the informer to start an argument. Then the guards could punish us for the quarrel by refusing to allow us to shower.

■ ■ ■

Under such harsh conditions, those of us who had faith in Christ realized for the first time how rich we were. Many of us Christians were young and physically weak. But we had more strength in suffering than the wealthiest older women and the smartest, strongest atheists.

With no books and concerts, the educated atheists seemed to shrivel up. They were like indoor plants exposed to harsh outdoor winds.

Women who had been wealthy were the most pitiful. Prison life was harder for them than for anyone else. They had lost the most possessions. And they had nothing on the inside to fill the gap. The rubble of fancy hats, luxury hotels, constant entertainment, and popular friends rattled around in their memories like junk in the trunk of a car.

"How happy you must be!" said one of the women to me. "You are able to think clearly, pray, and keep your mind busy!"

Women came to Christian prisoners for help. They begged to hear what we remembered from the Bible. The words gave them hope, comfort, and life.

We had no Bible. Christian prisoners hungered for one more than for bread.

Before my arrest, I knew it would soon be my turn to go to prison. So I had tried to learn many Bible passages by heart. Others had done the same. In this way, we brought riches to prison. How we wished we had memorized more when we had the chance!

But daily, we repeated what we did remember. At night, when we held prayer meetings, we recited our verses. When new Christians came, we learned the verses they brought, and we taught them what we knew. So the words of an unwritten Bible passed through all of Romania's prisons.

While others quarreled and fought, we rested on our bunks and "read" our Bibles.

■ ■ ■

The Romanian government wanted to build a **canal** to link the **Danube River** with the **Black Sea**. They decided to send prisoners to do the work.

Along with thousands of others, I was forced to work on the canal. It reminded me of my ancestors in Egypt who served as **Pharaoh**'s slaves.

For hours each day, women prisoners shoveled dirt into wheelbarrows. The men prisoners pushed the heavy wheelbarrows up a steep hill and dumped out the dirt. We were building an embankment.

The work was too hard for weak prisoners trying to survive on bad prison food. On Sundays, we longed for

Canal: A manmade waterway for boats.

Black Sea: A sea between Europe and Asia.

Danube River: A river in Europe that flows through Romania.

Pharaoh: A king of ancient Egypt, a country in northeast Africa. The Book of Exodus tells the story of the Jews' escape from slavery under a Pharaoh.

rest. Instead, we had to go to classes to learn more about communism.

Guards marched us to an assembly hall. A speaker stood at the front of the room. She began by telling us what she thought about God, which wasn't much.

"Outside of here, everyone is now a communist," she lied. "There are no more Christians. You are the only ones holding on to such silly beliefs. Anyone who speaks about God will be punished.

"Do not think of yourselves as prisoners," she continued. "Think of yourselves as students. You are not in prison; you are in school. We are teaching you how to be happy! By learning your lessons, you may get out sooner!"

After she spoke, singers and actresses put on a concert for us. They sang communist songs and recited communist poetry. One poem praised the Russians who brought communism to Romania:

"There are no more Christians. You are the only ones holding on to such silly beliefs."

Mother Russia, thank you
For what you've done today.
The glorious Red army
Has shown us all the way.

The guards commanded everyone to cheer loudly for the performers.

"Students" who showed no enthusiasm were thought to be "socially rotten." Informers watched closely for people who didn't clap or cheer.

I didn't applaud.

Other prisoners told me, "Pretend! What does it matter? Is it worth getting in trouble?"

I couldn't applaud when the performers denied God. I squeezed among the people standing at the back of the hall so I would be less noticeable.

But I didn't escape. Someone reported me. Guards marched me into the prison warden's office.

"I have information that you failed to clap at today's class," the warden said. "All your behavior here has shown that you are not learning your lessons. We've tried to be good to you. Now other methods will be used."

The guards put me in a closet so small that I could only stand. The iron door had a few air holes in it. I had to stand in the closet for hours.

I tried to think of ways to keep my mind busy. Drops of water fell on the roof of the closet. I counted them to make the time pass.

One: There is one God.

Two: The Ten Commandments were on two tablets.

Three: Three is for the Father, Son, and Holy Spirit.

Four: The Bible says Christ will gather His people from the four corners of the earth.

Five: Five is for the five Books of Moses.

Six: The number of the beast in Revelation is 666.

Seven: Seven is a holy number in the Bible.

When I ran out of numbers, I started over. I prayed and God gave me other ways to pass the time without giving in to despair.

■ ■ ■

The guards decided that our work on the canal was not going fast enough.

At a meeting, they called twenty women to the front of the room.

"You have been the hardest workers here!" the warden announced. "So we are setting you free!"

He praised their work and handed them each a loaf of bread as a gift. The women climbed into a truck, singing and waving red flags.

Ten miles down the road, the truck stopped at the next prison. The women were taken off the truck and put back to work. They were not free at all.

Back at our prison, we didn't know what had happened to them at first. We worked harder, hoping we, too, would soon be free. But this trick was performed at other prisons, and soon the truth got back to us.

■ ■ ■

Outside the prison at night, we heard the wind howling. It seemed to have blown all these strangers together: old and young, women of fashion and homeless beggars. All we had in common was suffering. Since we had this in common, I could be a friend with women who might not talk to me in freedom.

One such woman was Tania. Tania was an expert thief. She acted so proud of her ability to steal.

I found it difficult to talk to Tania about God. She just did not want to listen. But one day, maybe she really heard what I told her.

I said, "Tania, there are two worlds. One is the material world—the world of things. The other is the spiritual world.

"In the material world, the laws of God and man say, 'Do not steal.' But in the spiritual world, the rule is, 'Steal all you can.' You can steal knowledge, manners, and wisdom in the spiritual world.

"I have no problem with your being a thief. The trouble is that you don't know what to steal.

"Whatever you take in the material world, you will lose when you die—or sooner. But suppose you take the wisdom and knowledge of God from somebody. You will keep it for eternity."

Tania, like the rest of us, often went hungry. Yet she did not forget the birds. She hoarded crumbs from her bread and put them on the window sill for sparrows.

In every kind of criminal prisoner, I could find a small piece of goodness.

■ ■ ■

Sabina Imprisoned

At the canal, I met a boy name Marin Motza. He and his sister were in prison with their mother.

Marin was twelve years old—Mihai's age. Every time I saw Marin, I thought of Mihai.

Who was caring for my son? Was he following Christ? Did he have food to eat and clothes to keep him warm?

I must have prayed for him during every hour that I was awake, and I often dreamed about him.

CHAPTER 13

An Empty House

I felt like I lived in a glass bowl. Whatever happened to my family, everybody knew about it.

My father had made history when he gave the speech to religious leaders at the Parliament building. Romania is a small nation. The radio carried his speech to the whole country. Every Romanian knew the name Richard Wurmbrand.

But that didn't help me after my mother went to prison. In fact, it made things worse.

When people saw me on the street, they crossed to the other side and pretended not to know me. They were afraid of getting arrested. To the communists, being a friend of the Wurmbrands could be a crime.

■ ■ ■

It seemed like the whole country was one big prison. Even when we weren't locked up, it felt like we were. I heard about people who went to a government office to do something innocent like register their bicycle. Then the next thing they knew, they were taken to prison for no reason—just because a policeman at the office saw them and felt like arresting them.

People went to prison for doing absolutely nothing wrong.

A man in prison with my father told a story that he said was true:

The prison warden ordered a group of convicts to stand in line for an inspection.

As the warden strolled down the line, he asked each man the same question: "What is your crime?"

The first prisoner answered, "I've done nothing, sir, and I'm in prison for ten years."

The warden moved on.

"And what is your crime?" he asked another inmate.

"Nothing, sir," the prisoner answered. "And I'm serving twenty years."

"Liar!" thundered the warden. "Nobody in the People's Republic of Romania gets more than ten years for doing nothing!"

Maybe the story was true. Or maybe it was just a joke. But there was truth behind it. Innocent people often went to prison, and the communists knew they had done nothing to deserve punishment.

An Empty House

■ ■ ■

I was about eleven when Mother was arrested. After she left, there was no time to cry and no one to listen to me if I did.

Bucharest was filled with thousands of street children, living like ghosts in a ghost town. Whole blocks of houses stood empty because all the adults living there had been arrested.

I stayed by myself in our house for a while. Then the communists came and took almost all our property. My toys, my bed, all the other furniture—they dumped everything into the street, then carted it away.

Mother had a special Bible. It had been a present from my father. Every other page was blank. Mother had written her thoughts, prayers, and memories on the blank pages.

Some of the writing was in her own private code. If the communists saw it, they would be very suspicious. They would suspect that the coded words were anti-communist messages.

But I managed to keep the Bible away from the police. I hid my father's typewriter well, too. My parents were grateful for both when they returned.

■ ■ ■

I went to the home of a Christian woman I called Auntie Alice.

"You'll be my mom now," I said to her.

Alice was not really my aunt, and she could have refused to help me. She already cared for her elderly father in a one-room apartment. But she welcomed me and squeezed me into their lives.

Alice had an important job for the government. But as a Christian, she refused to join the Communist Party. So she was fired.

When I lived with Auntie Alice, we had trouble finding enough food. She earned a little money tutoring French and preparing students for high school graduation exams. Her father even got a job for a while so we could get a ration card.

We might have gone hungry if bold Christians hadn't helped us. A woman from a village hundreds of miles away heard about Mother's arrest. She traveled all the way to Bucharest to give me a sack of potatoes—all she had to offer.

Prison wasn't the only place informers did their work. There were informers everywhere. They watched people whose relatives were in prison for disagreeing with the communists.

An informer saw the woman give me the potatoes. When she got home, she was taken to the police station. The police treated her so roughly and scared her so badly that she never recovered her health.

After Mother got out of prison, the police took away Auntie Alice, too. They charged her with "harboring the child of political prisoners." She went to prison for six years.

An Empty House

■ ■ ■

I tried to visit my parents when they were in prison, but it wasn't easy. Some of the prisons were far from Bucharest.

Once I had to board a train in the middle of the night in the winter. I wanted to see my mother. After a long, cold, five-hour ride, the train got to a station near the prison at 6 a.m.

I got off the train along with family members of other prisoners. We walked for an hour in the snow to get to the prison.

Then we stood in the snow, waiting.

We stood for a very long time.

Nothing happened.

Finally we saw a long line of prisoners.

Suddenly a guard yelled, "Go home! No visit today! The prisoners did not obey orders well enough to have visitors!"

We walked back to the station, got on the train, and went home.

■ ■ ■

A few weeks later, I tried again. This time, I got to see my mother. But I had to wait all day. Visitors entered the visiting area in alphabetical order. I was last.

Mother and I only saw each other for a few minutes. We had to stand thirty feet apart and were not allowed to touch.

She looked tired and thin. It broke my heart to see her in such an awful place.

Mother called out to me across the space that separated us, "Mihai, believe in Jesus with all your heart!"

She was in prison, but she was worried about *me!* She thought I might be drifting away from God. She wondered if I was starting to believe the lies of the communists.

There was no need for her to worry. I knew that if she still loved Jesus in that horrible prison, He must be the true Savior. Even if Christianity had no other arguments in its favor than my mother's belief in it, that would have been enough for me. Only Christ can give the hope that would light such a dark place.

■ ■ ■

One of my father's prisons had been a castle. The guards let me pass through huge wooden doors in the outside wall. Inside, I walked through a yard and more big doors in another wall.

They led me to a room with a long table. Policemen sat on both sides of the table.

About fifteen feet away stood a big door with a window in it. A small sliding door covered the window.

I shivered and trembled nervously as I stood waiting by the policemen's table.

The sliding door opened and my father's face appeared in the window.

He looks older, I thought.

We knew visits could be very short. Father had time to ask only the most important questions and to say the most important things.

"How is your mother?" Father called out to me.

"You must not ask about family!" a policeman yelled before I could answer.

"How is my court case going?" Father asked.

"You are not allowed to ask about your case," a policeman said.

"Remember, Mihai," Father said quickly, "there is a God, Jesus is our Savior, and love is the best way."

The sliding door slammed shut.

■ ■ ■

Two years later, I visited Father again. Auntie Alice went with me.

When it was my turn to visit, a guard called out, "Mihai Wurmbrand!"

Father and I met in a large hall. He sat in a box with a window blocked by three iron bars. I sat in a chair facing Father's box. The window was so small I could see only part of his face.

I knew from experience that we might not get to talk much. So I gave him a message from Mother first.

"Mother says even if you die in prison you must not be sad because we'll all meet in heaven!" I said as fast as I could.

Father looked like he didn't know whether to laugh or cry. I realized later that my message probably wasn't very comforting. Maybe I should have greeted him with more hopeful words.

"How is she?" Father asked. "Do you have enough food?"

"She's okay," I answered. "And there is food at home. Our Father is very rich."

I saw the guard smiling. He didn't know I was talking about our Father God. If he had known, I might have been kicked out of the prison.

The guard smiled because he thought I had a new father. The communists tried to get wives of Christian prisoners to divorce their husbands. Then the prisoners might give up their faith—or so the communists thought.

Government officials had visited Mother and tried to force her to file for divorce. Of course, she would not even think about it.

■ ■ ■

After a while the police came looking for me. They said I had committed the crime of "**defrauding** the state." I owed the government thousands of dollars, they claimed.

> **Defraud:** To take or keep something by trickery or cheating.

An Empty House

Here is what had happened. When the police took all our belongings after Mother's arrest, they lied on their reports.

They had been ordered to make a list of items they took from us. Then they were supposed to give the items to the government.

Instead, when they took a chair, they wrote that they threw the chair away because it had only three legs. They said they got rid of the piano because it had no keyboard.

Actually, there was nothing wrong with our furniture. And the police hadn't thrown it away. They sold it and kept the money for themselves. But later they got caught.

The communists said the policemen's false report was my fault. The police had shown me the list of property that they took away, and they ordered me to sign it. I signed it without reading it. So the government said I helped the police to lie on the report!

I wrote my uncle in France for help in raising the money. As often as he could, he sent me raincoats to sell. Raincoats were valuable because they were rare in Romania, so I sold them for high prices. That's how I paid the government.

■ ■ ■

Later, Mother told me something that happened in prison. One day, the guards began to take women one by one to the prison offices. The officials asked the prisoners:

"Do you know how wrong you were to disagree with the government?"

"What do you think about the things you have learned in prison?"

"Do you agree that you needed to be in prison to learn the error of your ways?"

"Do you understand that nothing and no one will be able to stop the communists from ruling the world?"

Most of the prisoners wanted to avoid punishment and get out of prison. So they told the officials what they wanted to hear.

"Yes, I was wrong," they said. "I have learned much in prison. Nothing can stop communism."

Then it was Mother's turn. The official had some extra questions for her.

"Do you know that I am more powerful than God?" he asked. "Have you learned Christianity is fake? Do you know that God is not necessary in a communist society?"

Mother answered, "I see that you are powerful. You probably have documents there that tell everything about me and can decide my future. But God keeps records, too. Neither you nor I would have life without Him. So whether He keeps me in prison or sets me free, I will accept that as best for me."

The official banged his fists on his desk and shouted, "Ungrateful! You are ungrateful for what we have taught you! You have failed to learn your lesson. I will report that to my superiors!"

But three days later, Mother was released. More powerful authorities than the official were deciding her future.

An Empty House

■ ■ ■

A prison truck dropped Mother off in Bucharest. She walked to the home of a friend and knocked at the door.

"Sabina! Is it possible you are free?" exclaimed her astonished friend when she opened the door.

Someone came to find me and took me to Mother. As we hugged, she began to cry.

I wiped away her tears. "Don't cry, Mother. Please don't cry."

We had a big reunion among friends. I was very happy, but also angry with the people who had treated my mother so harshly.

"We should hate communism, but love the communists," she reminded me.

"Mother, that will be the hardest thing I've ever done," I replied.

It was never easy for me. But God gave us more opportunities to learn to love our enemies and forgive our persecutors in the following days, months, and years.

CHAPTER 14

A Surprise Reunion

In the spring of 1956, some swallows built a nest in the eaves of the roof outside my cell. One day, we heard a tiny *cheep, cheep*. The swallows' eggs had hatched.

One prisoner stood on another's shoulders to get a closer look out the window.

"Four of them!" he announced.

The parent birds never seemed to rest. Having nothing better to do, we decided to count their trips to and from the nest. In one day, they made 250 trips to feed their babies!

"They'll fly in twenty-one days," said a prisoner who used to be a farmer.

Other prisoners laughed at him.

"Birds can't read calendars!" they jeered.

"You'll see," the farmer said.

On the twentieth day, nothing seemed different in the swallows' lives. But on the twenty-first day, chirping and fluttering, the young birds flew.

Everyone smiled, even the roughest prisoners.

"God has arranged their schedule," I said. "He can do the same for us."

■ ■ ■

The government was releasing many prisoners. *Would I be one of them?* The thought made me sad.

If they let me go now, what use would I be to anybody? I thought. *Mihai probably doesn't need me. He's been without a father for eight and a half years. Sabina is used to living without a husband. The church has other pastors who cause less trouble than I would.*

■ ■ ■

One morning, a guard appeared suddenly at my cell and called my name.

"Hurry up! Move!" he shouted impatiently. "You're wanted for questioning."

I hurried with him down hallways and across the prison yard. One after another, steel gates were unlocked.

Then I stood outside.

No one questioned me. Instead, a clerk handed me a slip of paper. It was a court order. I was free.

I stared at the order, dazed.

A Surprise Reunion

All I could say was, "But I've served only eight and a half years, and my sentence is for twenty!"

"Leave *now!*" said the clerk. "The order comes from the highest level."

"I've got twelve more years to serve!"

"Don't argue! Get out!"

"But look at me!" I said.

My ragged shirt was filthy. My pants had patches everywhere. A string held them up at the waist. My shoes didn't fit.

"I'll be arrested by the first policeman who sees me looking like this!"

"We have no clothes here for you," the clerk said. "Please, just leave."

"God, help me not to rejoice more because I'm free than because You were with me in prison!"

The clerk went back into the prison. He shut and locked the gate.

The prison was three miles outside Bucharest. I looked around, but saw no one. A long, white road stretched past groves of trees. After years of being in colorless prisons, I was fascinated by all the green.

I called out loudly, so that the guards could hear behind their walls. "God, help me not to rejoice more because I'm free than because You were with me in prison!"

Then I set off across the fields. I walked in the deep grass and touched the rough bark of trees. Sometimes I stopped to gaze at a flower or a leaf.

Imprisoned for Christ

An old farmer and his wife walked toward me.

"Do you come from *there?*" the man asked, nodding toward the prison.

"Yes," I answered.

The man got a coin out of his pocket and gave it to me.

"Thank you," I said. "Please give me your address so I can repay you when I get home."

"No, no. You keep it," the couple urged.

I walked on. Another woman stopped me.

"Did you come from the prison?" she asked.

She hoped to find out if I had met a pastor from her village in prison. I had not met him, but I told her I was a pastor, too.

We sat on a wall by the roadside. I was happy to find someone who wanted to talk about Christ.

When we parted, she, too, gave me a coin.

"For your streetcar fare," she said.

"But I have one already," I protested.

"Take it for our Lord's sake then."

I walked on until I reached a streetcar stop. People crowded around me when they realized where I came from. They wanted news about brothers, fathers, and cousins. Everybody had a relative in prison.

When I boarded the streetcar, they wouldn't let me pay. Several people stood up to offer me a seat. Freed prisoners were highly respected.

Just as the streetcar started, I heard someone yelling from outside, "Stop! Stop!"

A Surprise Reunion

We jerked to a halt. A policeman's motorcycle swerved in front of the streetcar to block it.

There's been a mistake! I thought. *They've come to take me back to the prison!*

Sometimes prison officials played tricks like that.

The streetcar driver talked to the policeman. "He says there's someone standing on the steps," the driver told the passengers. "He's warning me not to allow it again."

What a relief!

Next to me sat a woman with a basket of fresh strawberries. I stared at them, amazed.

"Haven't you seen any strawberries yet this year?" she asked.

"Not for eight years," I said.

"Go on, take some!"

I ate them hungrily.

Finally, I reached my own front door. For a moment I hesitated. Then I opened the door.

■ ■ ■

Twice a year, I applied to the government for a pardon for Richard. Twice a year, they turned me down.

I knew there was little chance Richard would receive a pardon. But I still felt so disappointed when the refusals came in the mail.

In early 1956, I again filled out an application requesting that he be pardoned. Then I waited for the mailman to bring a reply.

■ ■ ■

A young girl had visited our church years before. She came from a Christian family but she was not really following Christ. Her brother, who loved the Lord, had invited her to church.

Later the girl, now a young woman, married a communist who became an assistant to the chief of the secret police. She still was not following Christ. But she often talked about her visit to our church.

"I never heard a sermon like the one Pastor Wurmbrand preached," she told her husband. "He's a very dynamic man."

The young communist wanted to impress his wife and his boss. So he thought of a plan.

He arranged to question my father. He hoped to get him to say something bad about communists. His boss could use what Father said against him. And his wife could see that he was smarter than the pastor she so admired.

So he went to the prison to question Father.

"Write down what you think of communists and communism," the man ordered him.

After a while, he returned to take what Father had written. He began reading it eagerly.

A Surprise Reunion

When he went home to his wife that evening, he told her about the meeting and about what Father had written.

"I have never met another prisoner like that!" he said. "He has been in a communist prison for eight and a half years. But he wrote about how much he loves his enemies. He said communists have empty hearts. He forgives us and isn't bitter!"

After reading what Father wrote about the love of Christ, the man changed his mind about wanting to cause him trouble.

One day, he brought his boss a stack of papers to sign. As he usually did, the boss signed them all without really looking at them. He trusted his assistant.

The man had written an order for Father to be freed, and slipped it into the stack. His boss signed it. It was a long time before we found out how God had used the man to free Father.

In the meantime...

■ ■ ■

 The official reply to my application for Richard's pardon arrived in the mail.

It said, "Your application for a pardon has been denied."

My husband came home that same day...

■ ■ ■

Imprisoned for Christ

When I opened the door, I saw a group of young people sitting and talking.

One tall, skinny young man stared at me, then burst out, "Father!"

Mihai was nine when I left; now he was eighteen.

Then my wife came forward—thinner and older, but more beautiful than ever. She was laughing and weeping. We embraced and I softly sang a little song I had composed for her years before in prison for if we ever met again on earth.

Our home soon filled with visitors. Members of our church had phoned all over Bucharest with the news that I was out. The doorbell rang continually.

Old friends brought new ones. People had to leave so others could find standing room.

Three of the visitors told me that my son had brought them to faith in Christ. And I had feared that he would be lost without a father or mother! I could find no words for my happiness.

I wanted to kiss my wife, even in front of all the visitors. But I had something important to say.

"Before we kiss," I said, "I must say something. Don't think I've simply come from misery to happiness. I've come from the joy of being with Christ in prison to the joy of being with Him in our family. I'm not coming from strangers to my family, but from my brothers in Christ in prison to my family in Christ at home."

A Surprise Reunion

■ ■ ■

Now that I was free, I longed for quiet and rest. But the enemies of Christ were fighting everywhere to destroy Christianity. Much work remained to be done in the underground church. I needed to get started immediately.

Epilogue

Pastor Wurmbrand *did* start serving the Lord in the Underground Church immediately. Three years later, he was again imprisoned for his faithful obedience to the Lord. Mrs. Wurmbrand and Mihai continued his secret work during the almost six years he was gone.

In 1964, Pastor Wurmbrand was released from prison. Christians helped the Wurmbrands to leave Romania. Romanian officials warned Pastor Wurmbrand to keep silent about the persecution of Christians in communist countries. He did not heed their warnings.

In 1967, the Wurmbrands started an organization in the United States called "Jesus to the Communist World." Its mission was to inform the world about suffering Christians, and to help persecuted believers. The name of the organization was later changed to "The Voice of the Martyrs." Today, The Voice of the Martyrs works in more than 50 countries.

In August 2000, Mrs. Wurmbrand went to be with the Lord. Pastor Wurmbrand died in February 2001 at the age of 91.

Rev. Michael (Mihai) Wurmbrand lives in California. Rev. Wurmbrand has traveled to Romania for The Voice of the Martyrs to locate and help families of former prisoners for the Lord. VOM helped provide for Mena, the woman who brought Mihai some potatoes (Chapter 13), until her death in the 1990s.

Timeline

1909	Richard Wurmbrand is born.
1913	Sabina is born.
1936	Richard and Sabina are married.
1938	Richard and Sabina dedicate their lives to Christ.
1939	Mihai is born.
1941	German Nazi soldiers take control of Romania.
1944	Russian communist soldiers drive the Nazis out.
1948	Pastor Wurmbrand is arrested.
1950	Mrs. Wurmbrand is arrested.
1953	Mrs. Wurmbrand is released.
1956	Pastor Wurmbrand is released.
1959	Pastor Wurmbrand is arrested.
1964	Pastor Wurmbrand is released.
1965	The Wurmbrands leave Romania.
1967	"Jesus to the Communist World" mission begins (later renamed The Voice of the Martyrs).
1989	Forty years of communist rule in Romania ends.
1990	The Wurmbrands return to Romania to visit.
2000	Mrs. Wurmbrand goes home to be with Jesus.
2001	Pastor Wurmbrand dies at the age of 91.

100 Ways to Help the Persecuted Church

Ways Kids Can Learn, Share, Pray

1. Design a church bulletin insert about persecution.

2. Make bookmarks for friends to remind them to pray for suffering Christians.

3. Write, record, and share a song about martyrs.

4. Help someone subscribe to a free VOM publication.

5. Commit to praying for one persecuted Christian for 30 days.

6. Start a group among your friends to learn about and pray for persecuted Christians.

7. Act out a scene from a book about persecuted Christians and videotape it to share.

8. Make a scrapbook of stories about persecuted Christians from VOM publications.

9. Make a poster listing these 100 Ways and display it at church.

10. Set up an exhibit table about persecution at church.

11. Donate VOM publications to a Christian school.

12. Hold a concert to raise funds for projects to help persecuted Christians.

13. Help your church observe the International Day of Prayer for the Persecuted Church.

14. Offer free VOM Special Issues to a Christian bookstore.

15. Share VOM resources with a Vacation Bible School director.

16. Offer to share in your Sunday school class about persecution.

17. When you are asked to pray in a group, remember the needs of the persecuted.

18. Compare the stories of Bible heroes to those of today's persecuted Christians.

19. Design a bumper sticker to raise awareness of persecuted Christians.

20. Pray for persecuted Christians you see featured in the news.

21. Make paper flags to reminder you to pray for countries where Christians are persecuted.

22. Write letters to missionaries or soldiers serving in countries hostile to Christians.

23. Visit the VOM online bookstore to shop for Christmas or birthday gifts.

24. Make a doorknob hanger as a reminder to pray for struggling Christians.

25. Send Bibles and other Christian books to VOM for shipment to restricted countries.

26. Make or buy a rubber stamp that says "Pray for [name of persecuted Christian]."

27. Share VOM videos or other resources with a youth pastor.

28. Use time waiting in checkout lines to pray for persecuted Christians.

29. Make a bracelet to remind you to pray for suffering Christians.

30. Buy a book about a martyr. Read it, then donate it to a library.

31. Make a computer mouse pad that reminds you to pray for suffering Christians.

32. Become an expert about a persecuted country. Offer to be interviewed about it on radio.

33. Laminate VOM newsletter pages to use as placemats.

34. When you are cold, sick, or in pain, pray for suffering Christians.

35. Make a prayer calendar featuring the needs of Christians at risk.

36. Put on a drama about suffering Christians.

37. Raise money to send a member of your group to a VOM conference.

38. Ask your elected officials if they would like information about persecuted Christians.

39. Start a lending library of materials about persecuted Christians.

40. Write a polite letter to a foreign embassy on behalf of persecuted Christians.

41. Offer a foreign language Bible to a visitor from a country where Bibles are rare. (To order the Bibles, visit www.multilanguage.com.)

42. Write a story about persecution and submit it to a magazine.

43. Share past issues of VOM publications with those who haven't read them.

44. Maintain a church bulletin board about persecution.

45. Make a paper chain with links containing the names of Christians to pray for.

46. Hold a bake sale or cooking contest to raise funds to help persecuted Christians.

47. Make a pamphlet about your project to share with friends who might help.

48. Write letters to persecuted Christians in prison. Visit the VOM website for information.

49. Use time riding in the car to pray for persecuted Christians.

50. Dress a mannequin like a Christian hero. Present that person's testimony to a group.

51. Attach pictures of persecuted Christians to a world map. Pray for them.

52. Collect stories about children living in restricted countries to share.

53. Start a neighborhood newspaper. Include VOM news.

54. Record your prayers for persecuted Christians in a prayer journal.

55. Using the Bible to help you, write a report about why Christians suffer.

56. Invite a speaker from a persecuted country to share with a group. Or, if one is not available, schedule a speaker from VOM.

57. On a map, draw a small cross on a country each time you pray for the people there.

58. Wear a VOM T-shirt or give one as a gift.

59. Put VOM publications in your doctor's waiting room.

60. Learn more about Islam and Muslim converts to Christ.

61. Make key rings using photos from VOM publications.

62. Help run a sport or game tournament to raise money to aid struggling Christians.

63. Write a poem about persecuted Christians and send it to a website or magazine.

64. Add a story about persecuted Christians to a website or blog.

65. Recycle cans to raise funds to help persecuted Christians.

66. Share stories of victorious Christians with someone who is discouraged.

67. Use time while running or exercising to pray for the persecuted.

68. Make a light switchplate cover with pictures of persecuted Christians, to serve as a prayer reminder.

69. Worship outside and remember those whose churches have been burned.

70. Learn some words in the language of a country where you want to minister someday.

71. Save the fronts of Christmas cards to use as postcards for Christians prisoners.

72. Design a poster or mural about Christians who have suffered for their faith.

73. Use Isaiah 41:10 and Psalm 107:19 as prayers for persecuted Christians.

74. Put on a puppet show about today's heroes of the faith.

75. Share about persecuted Christians at family meals or devotions.

76. Pray for persecutors to repent and follow Jesus.

77. Start a letter-writing club to write to Christian prisoners.

78. Send VOM resources to a U.S. prison chaplain to share with prisoners.

79. Have a car wash to earn funds for a project to help the persecuted.

80. Make a list of hymns about persecution for events where persecution is discussed.

81. Make a "Family Prayer Album" using clips from VOM publications.

82. Display items about persecution at a history or geography fair.

83. Leave a VOM publication in a car mechanic's waiting room

84. Find the names of leaders of restricted nations in an almanac. Pray for them.

85. Serve a dinner featuring food from a restricted country. Share about Christians there.

86. Make a parade float about courageous Christians.

87. Phone a friend once a week to pray together for persecuted Christians.

88. Design Christmas ornaments using photos from VOM publications.

89. Hold an overnight lock-in, and spend the time learning about and praying for persecuted Christians.

90. Collect spare change in a jar for a year to support a VOM project.

91. Write a book report on a book about persecuted Christians.

92. Plan to pray for Christians in Muslim countries during Muslim holidays.

93. Hold a weekly or monthly fast from TV, computer games, or dessert as a prayer reminder.

94. Write a letter to the editor of a publication, telling about current persecution.

95. Study Bible passages about persecution and share them with someone.

96. Send profits from a lemonade stand or garage sale to support VOM projects.

97. Offer to show a video about persecution to a group or class.

98. Hold an "underground church service." Sing and pray quietly.

99. Invite party guests to bring items needed by the persecuted instead of gifts.

100. Send a description of your projects to VOM to share with others.

Bible References

Verses cited or mentioned in the text are listed below.

Chapter 1

Draw near to God and He will draw near to you. Cleanse your hands, you sinners; and purify your hearts, you double-minded. *(James 4:8)*

Chapter 2

But God demonstrates His own love toward us, in that while we were still sinners, Christ died for us. *(Romans 5:8)*

Chapter 3

Is anyone among you sick? Let him call for the elders of the church, and let them pray over him, anointing him with oil in the name of the Lord. *(James 5:14)*

But if we walk in the light as He is in the light, we have fellowship with one another, and the blood of Jesus Christ His Son cleanses us from all sin. *(1 John 1:7)*

"You have a few names even in Sardis who have not defiled their garments; and they shall walk with Me in white, for they are worthy. He who overcomes shall be clothed in white garments, and I will not blot out his name from the

Book of Life; but I will confess his name before My Father and before His angels." *(Revelation 3:4,5)*

Chapter 4

Then they drew near to the village where they were going, and He indicated that he would have gone farther. But they constrained Him, saying, "Abide with us, for it is toward evening, and the day is far spent." And He went in to stay with them. *(Luke 24:28,29)*

He answered and said to them, "He who has two tunics, let him give to him who has none; and he who has food, let him do likewise." *(Luke 3:11)*

Chapter 5

For God did not send His Son into the world to condemn the world, but that the world through Him might be saved. *(John 3:17)*

"Beware of false prophets, who come to you in sheep's clothing, but inwardly they are ravenous wolves." *(Matthew 7:15)*

Chapter 6

So it came to pass, when they had brought them outside, that he said, "Escape for your life! Do not look behind you nor stay anywhere in the plain. Escape to the mountains, lest you be destroyed." *(Genesis 19:17)*

"For whoever desires to save his life will lose it, but whoever loses his life for My sake will find it." *(Matthew 16:25)*

Chapter 8
My brethren, let not many of you become teachers, knowing that we shall receive a stricter judgment. *(James 3:1)*

"But whoever causes one of these little ones who believe in Me to stumble, it would be better for him if a millstone were hung around his neck, and he were thrown into the sea." *(Mark 9:42)*

And it shall come to pass that whoever calls on the name of the Lord shall be saved. *(Acts 2:21)*

It is He who sits above the circle of the earth, and its inhabitants are like grasshoppers, who stretches out the heavens like a curtain, and spreads them out like a tent to dwell in. *(Isaiah 40:22)*

He stretches out the north over empty space; He hangs the earth on nothing. *(Job 26:7)*

But sanctify the Lord God in your hearts, and always be ready to give a defense to everyone who asks you a reason for the hope that is in you, with meekness and fear.
(1 Peter 3:15)

"And it shall come to pass that whoever calls on the name of the Lord shall be saved." *(Acts 2:21)*

Chapter 9

Blessed are you when men hate you, and when they exclude you, and revile you, and cast out your name as evil, for the Son of Man's sake. Rejoice in that day and leap for joy! For indeed your reward is great in heaven. For in like manner their fathers did to the prophets. *(Luke 6:22,23)*

To them it was revealed that, not to themselves, but to us they were ministering the things which now have been reported to you through those who have preached the gospel to you by the Holy Spirit sent from heaven—things which angels desire to look into. *(1 Peter 1:12)*

Chapter 11

For He made Him who knew no sin to be sin for us, that we might become the righteousness of God in Him. *(2 Corinthians 5:21)*

Rejoice with those who rejoice, and weep with those who weep. *(Romans 12:15)*

If a brother or sister is naked and destitute of daily food, and one of you says to them, "Depart in peace, be warmed and filled," but you do not give them the things which are needed for the body, what does it profit? Thus also faith by itself, if it does not have works, is dead. *(James 2:15–17)*

"But I say to you, love your enemies, bless those who curse you, do good to those who hate you, and pray for those who spitefully use you and persecute you." *(Matthew 5:44)*

Chapter 12

And take the helmet of salvation, and the sword of the Spirit, which is the word of God. *(Ephesians 6:17)*

So the Egyptians made the children of Israel serve with rigor. And they made their lives bitter with hard bondage—in mortar, in brick, and in all manner of service in the field. All their service in which they made them serve was with rigor. *(Exodus 1:13,14)*

"Hear, O Israel: The LORD our God, the LORD is one!" *(Deuteronomy 6:4)*

So He declared to you His covenant which He commanded you to perform, the Ten Commandments; and He wrote them on two tablets of stone. *(Deuteronomy 4:13)*

For there are three that bear witness in heaven: the Father, the Word, and the Holy Spirit; and these three are one. *(1 John 5:7)*

He will set up a banner for the nations, and will assemble the outcasts of Israel, and gather together the dispersed of Judah from the four corners of the earth. *(Isaiah 11:12)*

Here is wisdom. Let him who has understanding calculate the number of the beast, for it is the number of a man: His number is 666. *(Revelation 13:18)*

"You shall not steal." *(Exodus 20:15)*

The Voice of the Martyrs

The Voice of the Martyrs is a Christian organization that serves persecuted Christians around the world. VOM has five main purposes:

1. To encourage Christians to obey the Great Commission (Matthew 28:19) in areas of the world where Christians are persecuted for spreading the gospel of Jesus Christ. VOM helps Christians do this by providing Bibles, radio broadcasts, medical help, and other forms of aid.

2. To give relief to families of persecuted Christians in these areas of the world.

3. To help Christians who live in these areas win persecutors to Christ.

4. To aid Christians in countries that used to be controlled by communists.

5. To tell the world about the suffering, faith, and courage of persecuted Christians.

Kids of Courage (KOC) is a quarterly newsletter for students ages 5 to 13. *KOC* teaches students about courageous Christians around the world, and offers ways to help them.

For more information:

Call: 800-747-0085
Write: VOM, P.O. Box 443, Bartlesville, OK 74005-0443
Email: thevoice@vom-usa.org
Log on to: www.persecution.com, www.kidsofcourage.com